# DOWN,
## BUT NOT
# OUT

### How to Get Up
### When Life Knocks You Down

## WAYNE A. MACK

P U B L I S H I N G
P.O. BOX 817 • PHILLIPSBURG • NEW JERSEY 08865-0817

© 2005 by Wayne A. Mack

*Page design by Kirk DouPonce, Dog Eared Design*
*Typesetting by Lakeside Design Plus*

Printed in the United States of America

**Library of Congress Cataloging-in-Publication Data**

Mack, Wayne A.
    Down, but not out : how to get up when life knocks you down /
Wayne A. Mack ; foreword by Richard Mayhue.
        p. cm.—(Strength for Life)
    Includes bibliographical references and index.
    ISBN 0-87552-672-1 (paper)
        1. Worry—Religious aspects—Christianity. 2. Burn out
(Psychology)—Religious aspects—Christianity. 3. Depression,
Mental—Religious aspects—Christianity. 4. Pastoral counseling.
5. Christian life. I. Title.

    BV4908.5.M33 2005
    248.8'6—dc22
                                                    2004062804

# CONTENTS

# FOREWORD

In life, there are two kinds of certainties. If you are the breadwinner in your home, you might appreciate the certainty that, no matter how long or how hard you shop for an item, the day after you have bought it, the article will be on sale somewhere else cheaper. Dad, you'll remember you forgot to put the trash out front only when the garbage truck is two doors away and you are in the shower. For Mom there is the certainty that the bread will fall with the peanut-butter-and-jelly side down on the carpet. Young people can identify with the certainty that it won't be until you return home from the dinner party that you realize that you have a string of spinach stuck between your front teeth.

Let me add one more certainty about life—a serious certainty. "For man is born for trouble, as sparks fly upward" (Job 5:7). Neither you nor I will live a trouble-free or without-problems kind of life. Regardless of how effective the latest technological advances might be or what sophisticated advances might be made in the world of medicine, we will surely face throughout our lives the kinds of serious troubles that bump us off stride or even violently knock us to the ground. The issue is not "if," but "when." The question is, "How will you and I respond?" Will we be down-and-out for the count? Or is there a way to get back on our feet and live another day?

To this inevitable and much-feared certainty, Dr. Wayne Mack adds a brighter certainty—the certainty that God through His precious Word can reclaim, remake, revitalize, and restore us, no matter how serious or seemingly insolvable our personal situation or problems might be. One of the great declarations of Scripture reads, "If God is for us, who is against us?" (Rom. 8:31).

Dr. Mack brilliantly turns our gaze away from self and troubles to rivet our attention on the dazzling majesty of God. He redirects attention from failed human solutions to the infallible Word of God. This helpful volume exudes Dr. Mack's never-ending love for and inexhaustible confidence in God's truth revealed in Scripture. This book does not float one more theory in an endless barrage of theories on how to solve life's problems. Rather, it points to the certainty of God's eternal truth as the absolute basis by which to live.

I commend Dr. Mack for his unswerving confidence and unshakable trust in the practical reliability and sufficiency of the Bible. With enthusiasm, I recommend that you take the doctor's advice on how to recover from the predictable trouble in your life. That way, on your worst day, you might be down but you won't be out. And in the process, God's refining fire will have burned away more of the dross and tempered the metal of your soul to be stronger in the next battle.

Richard Mayhue, Th.D.
Executive Vice President
The Master's College and Seminary

# ACKNOWLEDGMENTS

Many people have been involved in helping me bring this book to fruition. To them I owe a great debt of gratitude. Without their help, in the midst of a very busy schedule, this book would have never come into existence. As you read the book, you may find some mistakes, in that I haven't been inspired as the biblical writers were. You may also find that the style is not as scintillating as you would like it to be. Please blame any negative thing about the book on me and give these dear people who helped me the credit for any of the positives. They have been of immense help in birthing this book.

Who are these people? Again, as in other books, credit must be given to Janet Dudek, who was initially responsible for typing and editing the contents. She spent many hours at this task. Her skill at helping me condense and phrase the material, her dedication, hard work, and support were invaluable. Her husband Jeff, an English teacher, looked over her shoulder (and figuratively speaking, mine as well) and gave valuable critique of grammar and style.

My wife Carol did her usual thing—reading the manuscript, making comments on better ways of stating the information, and then helping in developing the study questions at the end of each chapter. And, oh yes, I also want to thank our daughter Beth, who read the manuscript and gave some assistance through editing and making valuable suggestions.

I am also very grateful to Dr. Richard Mayhue, executive vice president of The Master's College and Seminary and a frequently published author, for being willing to read the book in manuscript form and then write a foreword for it.

Thanks to all these people, but especially thanks to God for His goodness and for His giving me something to write about. I pray that this book will be used mightily to bring glory to our Triune God and great blessing to His people for whom Christ died and rose again.

# INTRODUCTION

*Down, but Not Out* was written for the purpose of helping people handle some of the problems of life that
could be classified as "downers," experiences in life that rob
people of their joy and cause them much pain and distress. In
a book this size, we cannot, of course, address all the downer
problems that people experience, but we are going to focus
on some very common ones that many people struggle with
at some point in their lives. The first giant that we will tackle
is worry or anxiety. Other downers we will look at are the
problem of spiritual burnout, perplexity and confusion (not
knowing what to do), discouragement, discontentment, hopelessness, and feeling sorry for oneself.

This book is related to another book I wrote (with Joshua
Mack) called *God's Solutions to Life's Problems.* In that earlier
book the foundation for addressing life's problems God's way
was laid. In future books I hope to write about God's solutions to several other very common problems, including pride,

depression, the problem of pain and suffering, anger, impatience, and loneliness.

In life we inevitably encounter many uncertainties, but of this we can be sure: as long as we are in this world, *we will have problems.* Jesus promised that this would be the case: "In the world you [will] have tribulation" (John 16:33). Jacob's response when Pharaoh asked how many years he had lived illustrates this truth: "The years of my sojourning are one hundred and thirty; few and unpleasant have been the years of my life" (Gen. 47:9). The words of Job's friend Eliphaz in Job 5:7 also remind us of this reality. Eliphaz rightly said, "For man is born for trouble, as sparks fly upward." Moses, writing by inspiration of the Holy Spirit, presents the same perspective: "As for the days of our life, . . . their pride is but labor and sorrow" (Ps. 90:10).

Traveling through life, we will experience labor and sorrow, trouble and unpleasantries, problems and difficulties. These things are certainties in this world. They simply can't be avoided. And as we face these problems in life, it is also certain that we will often be tempted to or actually will get down about them in the various ways described in this book. Scripture and life experience illustrate the negative impact these downers tend to have on us.

Along with the certainties I have just mentioned, I'm glad to say there is fortunately another thing of which we can be sure, namely, that God has provided in Christ and in His Word wonderful solutions to the problems we face. After warning us that we would have problems in this world, Jesus gave us assurance: "But take courage; I have overcome the world" (John 16:33). God expects us to overcome our problems because He has given us the means to do it. Jesus overcame the world, and by His power at work within us, we can as well.

In 1 Corinthians 10:13 Paul said that for every problem we face, there is a way of escape so that we may be able to bear it. In Romans 8:35–39 Paul listed some of the problems that we can expect to face: persecution, lack of food, physical dangers, poverty, death, demonic opposition, things in the present and in the future, and struggles with principalities and powers. This list was not given for the purpose of encouraging despair; it was given for the purpose of proclaiming our great hope! "But in all these things we overwhelmingly conquer through Him who loved us. For I am convinced that [nothing] . . . will be able to separate us from the love of God, which is in Christ Jesus our Lord" (Rom. 8:37–39).

For those who follow sports, consider the significant difference in these two victories: one, the home team wins by two points, and two, the home team wins by fifty points. In both games the home team wins, but in the second game they overwhelmingly conquer. Paul has promised us that in Christ we will overwhelmingly conquer! Not only that, but regardless of the kind of opposition that we face—physical or spiritual, great or small—we can overcome. In Christ *all the downer problems* can be solved.

According to God's Word, there is a distinctly God-ordained way of solving life's problems. In this and our other books on this subject, we study *God's* solutions to life's problems. Proverbs 14:12 warns, "There is a way which seems right to a man, but its end is the way of death." Unbelievers have come up with all sorts of solutions to life's problems. They have devised strategies for handling worry and anxiety. They have techniques for handling discouragement, discontentment, hopelessness, and feeling sorry for oneself. There are books, television shows, radio programs, videotapes, and lecture series dedicated to handling problems according to man's wisdom.

As believers, we should not be concerned about man's wisdom for solving life's problems, but rather with God's wisdom for handling life's problems. In 2 Peter 1:3–4 God says that "His divine power has granted to us everything pertaining to life and godliness, through the true knowledge of Him who called us by His own glory and excellence. For by these He has granted to us His precious and magnificent promises, so that by them you may become partakers of the divine nature, having escaped the corruption that is in the world by lust."

In Christ we have been given everything that we need for living (handling the downers we face in daily life) and everything we need for godliness (handling the challenges that are connected to our relationship with God). First Corinthians 10:13 teaches, "No temptation has overtaken you but such as is common to man; and God is faithful, who will not allow you to be tempted beyond what you are able, but with the temptation will provide the way of escape also, so that you will be able to endure it." There is no problem in this world that God has not given us the power to overcome.

In 2 Timothy 3:16–17 God teaches us the place that His Word should have in addressing the problems in our lives: "All Scripture is given by inspiration of God, and is profitable for doctrine, for reproof, for correction, for instruction in righteousness, that the man of God may be complete, thoroughly equipped for every good work" (NKJV). We can be complete and thoroughly equipped for every good work! Everything that we need to face and handle the problems and challenges of life is contained in God's Word. This book is written to provide the direction and resources we need to handle the downers of life properly and productively. So as you read this book, I invite you to join with me in discovering the wonderful solutions God has given to us in His Word for facing and overcoming life's problems. God says, "There is a way of escape for every trial and testing." Let's dig in and together find those solutions for us and for our ministries to others.

# Part 1

# WORRY

## PUBLIC ENEMY NUMBER ONE

# 1

## THE SERIOUSNESS
## OF THE PROBLEM

One well-known Christian leader has called anxiety or worry "Public Enemy Number One." You may not agree that worry deserves the number-one rating. When you think of our Public Enemy Number One, you may want to give that rating to a problem such as heart disease, AIDS, terrorism, a struggling economy, or our national drug epidemic. However, while anxiety may not receive the Public Enemy Number One rating in your book, I'm sure you would still agree that it is a very serious problem with many people, perhaps even with you.

You ask if I might be exaggerating the seriousness of worry. What proof is there that worry is such a serious problem? Well, here are several evidences that demonstrate that worry should be considered a truly dangerous enemy, perhaps even Public Enemy Number One.

Let's think back over the last week, or even the last day. How many of us could honestly say that we have not worried about anything in that period of time? Perhaps it was about small things—what someone thinks of us, how some project will get finished on time, or whether the next bill will beat the next paycheck. Or perhaps it was about some very big things— what career move to make, how to deal with a crumbling marriage, or whether terrorists will strike again.

Some time ago, *Time* magazine termed the age in which we now live "The Age of Anxiety." It has been said that the epitaph "Hurry, Worry, Bury" would be appropriate on many tombstones these days because it so aptly describes many of our lives. It has been said that if the insignia of our forefathers was calloused hands, the insignia of modern-day man is a furrowed brow.

## WORRY: A COMMON AND SERIOUS PROBLEM

Truly, fear and anxiety is serious because *it is such a common—almost universal—problem in our world*, and that is undoubtedly why God has so much to say about it. Throughout the Bible we find many commands and encouragements regarding worry. We will look at many of those passages in this and the next two chapters, as well as some of the people in Scripture who had a problem with worry.

The problem of worry is serious because it is so universal, but it is also serious because God says that *it is a sin*. When most people think about sin, they think about stealing, swearing, lying, sexual immorality, or murder, but rarely do people think of worry as a sin. Or, if they recognize it as sin, they consider it to be a far less serious sin than these others are—hardly even worth mentioning. In fact, if we were to ask most believers to name some common sins, I doubt that many of them would even think of the sin of worry.

Why is this? The truth is, we tend to think that worry is a given in life, something that is natural or even integral to the human psyche. Indeed, humanist sociologists would tell us that anxiety served an important purpose in the evolution of man. Thus, we find it easy to excuse, minimize, and even make jokes about it. We hardly regard it as a sin against God.

## Worry Is Disobedience to God

The Bible, however, clearly teaches that worry is an act of disobedience against God. In Matthew 6:25–34 Jesus said three times, "Do not worry." This was not intended to be a suggestion for us to follow when—or if—we feel like it; this was given as a command! As we know, breaking a command of God is sin. Again, in John 14 Jesus commanded twice, "Do not let your heart be troubled" (14:1, 27). And by the inspiration of God's Holy Spirit, Paul wrote, "Be anxious for nothing" (Phil. 4:6). In light of these and similar commands in Scripture, we must regard worry and anxiety as a serious sin, not merely a weakness of character or human foible.

We also know that worry is serious because the Bible indicates that *worry has serious consequences.* Consider Abraham, who twice lied about the fact that Sarah was his wife (Gen. 12 and 20). Why did he lie? Though Abraham was called the father of the faithful in Scripture, he had a sinful, deceitful heart just as we do (Jer. 17:9), and Jesus taught us that what comes out of our mouths reveals what is in our hearts (Matt. 12:34). But Abraham's lie was not just a result of his deceitful heart; Abraham was worried and fearful.

The Scripture says that he was worried for his life because his wife was very beautiful. He called Sarah his sister so that no one would try to kill him in order to take her. Abraham sinned in his deceit, but the root of his problem was anxiety. That anxiety led him into more sin—deceiving Pharaoh and Abimelech—and the consequences of that sin—plagues on Pharaoh's house, a quick escort out of Egypt, and barren wombs in Abimelech's household. Worry has serious consequences.

Likewise, Saul experienced the consequences of worry. He was jealous and worried about David's growing popularity in the kingdom of Israel. He did some very nasty things to David because of his anxiety, causing much unnecessary trouble for himself and his kingdom. Saul pursued David into the wilderness, had eighty-five priests of the Lord murdered, and rejected his son Jonathan, among other things, because he was worried about the Israelites, thinking that David was greater than he was.

Proverbs 12:25 says, "Anxiety in a man's heart weighs it down." This verse reveals an important and common consequence of worry: depression. Like Siamese twins, anxiety and depression are often closely linked. People who are depressed are usually people who are experiencing a great amount of anxiety. In Luke 12 Jesus taught that worry leads to doubt and discouragement and motivates people to find relief in earthly treasures and earthly distractions. In 1 Peter 5 Peter said that worry opens the door for Satan to devour us. In Luke 8 and Mark 4 (the parable of the sower) Jesus taught that anxiety crowds out the Word of God in our lives, making us spiritually unfruitful.

In Proverbs 14:30 God said, "A tranquil heart is life to the body, but passion"—which includes anxiety—"is rottenness to the bones." Many people experience physical problems because of the anxiety in their hearts. When I taught a biblical counseling course some years ago, one of my students was the chief surgeon of the gastrointestinal unit of a large local hospital. At one point during the course, he came up to me and said that the problems of at least 80 percent of his patients could be traced to an inability to handle fear and anxiety.

The physical effects of anxiety are widely known in the medical community. In his book *None of These Diseases* S. I. McMillan lists at least sixty diseases that are caused or aggravated by inner turmoil. I have counseled many people whose struggle with anxiety has directly caused physical problems. I once worked with a man who lost forty pounds very quickly because his stomach was so upset from anxiety that he had constant indigestion. I counseled another man who was tired all the time. He went through all sorts of physical tests, but the doctors found nothing physically wrong. We found out that the reason he was tired was that he was so worried that he hardly ever slept more than four hours a night.

Indeed, worry is a serious problem because it has serious consequences. It can destroy our health, and it often destroys our happiness as well. Jesus rebuked Martha for being "worried and bothered about so many things" (Luke 10:41) when she complained about Mary's not being as consumed with preparations as she was. Like depression, a complaining spirit often accompanies anxiety. People who are always worried find it easy to complain because they are never satisfied with themselves or their circumstances, and they want to talk about it with anyone who will listen. Many people who come to me for counseling admit that they have few friends. I often discover that the reason for this is that they are always complaining, and other people find it difficult to listen for very long.

Another consequence of worry is that it hinders our usefulness. There are some very intelligent people who do poorly in school because of what has been termed "performance anxiety." Though they study hard and know the material, the pressure of a test causes such anxiety that they are unable to remember what they learned. Performance anxiety causes problems in other areas of achievement as well, such as athletics, music, and public speaking.

For example, I remember the first time that I ever preached in church. It was shortly after I had become a Christian, and I was only seventeen years old. At that point in my Christian life, I was really far too immature to be preaching to anyone, but since I had been asked and didn't know any better, I agreed. I put together a sermon that I estimated would take about forty-five minutes to deliver, but I was so nervous that I finished in about fifteen minutes. Or consider the man who got up to preach his "memorized" sermon and was so overcome by anxiety that he forgot it entirely. After a few moments of silence, he finally said, "Before I came here to preach, only the Lord and I knew what I was going to say. Now, only the Lord knows." Anxiety can inhibit our usefulness.

## WORRY IS USELESS AND UNNECESSARY

Worry is serious because it has serious consequences. It is also serious because *it is useless and unnecessary.* This was the point that Jesus was making in Matthew 6:27 when He asked, "And who of you by being worried can add a single hour to his life?" Indeed, worrying about how long we will live and when we will die will not change the length of our life or the day of our death. In Matthew 6:28–29 the Lord said, "And why are you worried about clothing? Observe how the lilies of the field grow; they do not toil nor do they spin." Worrying about clothes does not put them on our backs, and worrying about food does not put it on the table. Worry is a complete waste of time and energy because it will never cause something to happen or keep it from happening.

## WORRY IS UNBECOMING

Worry is also a serious problem because *it is unbecoming for a child of God.* It is not appropriate for believers to worry because of what our worry says about our Father. In Matthew 6:31–32 Jesus counseled, "Do not worry then, saying, 'What will we eat?' or 'What will we drink?' or 'What will we wear for clothing?' For the Gentiles eagerly seek all these things; for your heavenly Father knows that you need all these things." When Christians are anxious, they are a poor testimony to the world about their heavenly Father. Jesus said, "So do not be like them" (Matt. 6:8). In other words, do not be like unbelievers, who worry about all these things.

In Matthew 6:24 Jesus said, "No one can serve two masters; for either he will hate the one and love the other, or he will be devoted to one and despise the other. You cannot serve both God and wealth." When we worry about material things, we are making ourselves servants of those things. But God commands us to serve Him, not wealth. Worry is a poor testimony to the world about God's promise of provision for His children and about who our true Master is.

## Worry Involves Unbelief

Yet another reason that worry is serious is that *it is a result of unbelief.* In Matthew 6:30 Jesus said, "But if God so clothes the grass of the field, which is alive today and tomorrow is thrown into the furnace, will He not much more clothe you? You of little faith!" We worry because we do not believe that God will provide as He has promised. In fact, we are expressing doubt about God's truthfulness. But in Philippians 4:19 Paul gave us this promise: "God will supply all your needs according to His riches in glory in Christ Jesus."

In Matthew 6:33 Jesus promised, "But seek first His kingdom and His righteousness, and all these things will be added to you." If we fulfill our responsibility to seek first the kingdom of God and the righteousness of God, we have a promise from Him that He will give us everything that we need. When we choose to worry, we are essentially saying to God, "Lord, I don't believe Your promises." Our unbelief questions God's truthfulness.

Our unbelief also questions God's sovereignty. In Psalm 103:19 David said, "The LORD has established His throne in the heavens, and His sovereignty rules over all." Daniel 4:35 teaches, "But He does according to His will in the host of heaven and among the inhabitants of earth; and no one can ward off His hand or say to Him, 'What have You done?' " Not only can we be sure that God is in control, but we can also be sure that God is bringing it all about for our good. "And we know that God causes all things to work together for good to those who love God" (Rom. 8:28). When we worry, we question God's sovereignty because we do not believe that He is really in control.

Further, our anxiety shows unbelief in God's sincerity. Second Corinthians 1:20 teaches, "For as many as are the promises of God, in Him they are yes; therefore also through Him is our Amen." Hebrews 13:5–6 advises "being content with what you have; for He Himself has said, 'I will never desert you, nor will I ever forsake you,' so that we confidently say, 'The Lord is my helper, I will not be afraid. What will man do to me?' " When we worry, we are expressing doubt about the sincerity of God's promises. We really do not believe that He will do what He has promised to do.

Finally, our worry expresses unbelief in God's sufficiency. An anxious believer is someone who does not think that God is enough. In Isaiah 41:10 God pledged, "Do not fear, for I am with you. Do not anxiously look about you, for I am your God. I will strengthen you, surely I will help you, surely I will uphold you with My righteous right hand." Do we need more help than this? Is there a greater source of power? Can we find more comfort, or better provision, or freer grace? Truly, we cannot. God is more than sufficient for all our needs, and when we worry, we show our lack of faith in that sufficiency. We do not believe that He is enough.

Worry is a serious problem because it expresses unbelief, but it is also a serious problem because *it is an attempt to usurp the sovereignty of God.* In a sense, when we worry, we are trying to think and act like God, to put ourselves in control. In Numbers 11:10 we are told that Moses, the great servant of God, was "displeased." In the context of events, that word indicates that he was frustrated, discouraged, a bit angry, but also worried and fearful. In the next few verses, Moses complained to God that he could not do everything by himself. "I alone am not able to carry all this people, because it is too burdensome for me" (11:14). Moses was having a hard time, overwhelmed by anxiety and frustration, because he was trying to be God.

When we are anxious, it is often because we think that events are *out of* control, and not only that, but also that these events should be in *our* control. If we are facing a situation that we know is too much for us, but we think that we should be able to handle it, we become anxious. We feel responsible for making others act, for causing things to run smoothly, and for the outcome of events. In essence, we are aspiring to be God and frustrated because we are not.

Anxiety is an evidence of the pride in our hearts. We are not content to simply do what God commands and then leave the results to Him. Peter reminded us of the link between anxiety and pride in 1 Peter 5:6–7: "Therefore *humble yourselves* under the mighty hand of God, that He may exalt you at the proper time, *casting all your anxiety on Him*, because He cares for you." Proud people think that *they* have to make things happen, and they get anxious when things go differently than they planned. Peter urged us to stop thinking this way and to remember that God cares for us. He is trustworthy, sovereign, sincere, and sufficient.

## UNDERSTANDING WORRY AS GOD DOES

Now that we have considered all of these things, it is clear that anxiety is a very serious problem. It is important for us to view this problem correctly because how we view the problem of anxiety—with God's eyes or with man's eyes—will affect the way in which we address it. I have known people who sincerely believed that worry was a way of life for them. "Once a worrywart, always a worrywart." That is man's wisdom, not God's wisdom. It is very dangerous to view anxiety with the wisdom of this world.

The wisdom of this world provides many explanations for the existence of anxiety. According to the "nature" theory, some people are just born with a "sanguine" disposition. In other words, they are naturally cheerful, happy-go-lucky, and relatively free from worry. Others are born with a "melancholic" disposition. They are worriers by nature and thus doomed to a life of anxiety. On the other hand, those who favor the "nurture" theory believe that children who are raised in peaceful homes by peaceful parents will grow up to be free of anxiety.

Other children, raised in an atmosphere of fear, abuse, and deprivation, become adults whose lives are plagued by worry.

## WORRY CAN BE OVERCOME

Are we really doomed to the consequences of nature or nurture—or anything else? By God's grace, the answer to this question is No! The good news, according to God's infallible Word, is that the problem of worry can be overcome. As believers, we have the means to experience deep, satisfying, abiding peace in Christ Jesus. How can we be sure of this? Consider what the Scripture says.

Jeremiah 17:7–8 says, "Blessed is the man who trusts in the LORD and whose trust is the LORD. For he will be like a tree planted by the water, that extends its roots by a stream and will not fear when the heat comes; but its leaves will be green, and it will not be anxious in a year of drought nor cease to yield fruit." Psalm 29:11 promises, "The LORD will bless His people with peace." In Psalm 85:8 we read, "For He will speak peace to His people, to His godly ones." Isaiah 26:3 tells us, "The steadfast of mind You will keep in perfect peace, because he trusts in You."

Galatians 5:22 tells us where this peace comes from: "But the fruit of the Spirit is . . . peace." Anxiety is the fruit of a sinful heart, but God's peace is the fruit of His Spirit. In Philippians 4:6 Paul commands, "Be anxious for nothing." Paul is telling us that there is *never* a situation in life that necessitates or requires worry. There is never a social situation, financial situation, medical situation—there is no conceivable circumstance—in which we need to worry. "Be anxious for nothing."

We noted earlier that Jesus commanded, "Do not worry." Since we know that God does not ask us to do anything that He has not given us the power to do, we can be sure that *it is possible* to not be worried about anything. All of God's people can overcome the problem of worry. Philippians 4:7 reveals to us four important aspects of defeating anxiety in our lives: "And the *peace of God*, which *surpasses all comprehension*, will *guard* your hearts and your minds *in Christ Jesus*."

First, real peace is God's peace. It is not the peace of a happy-go-lucky disposition or a pleasant childhood. Overcoming anxiety requires the *peace of God*.

Second, real peace is peace that *surpasses all comprehension*. In other words, we cannot fully understand or explain this kind of peace because it is not based on anything tangible. In Psalm 3:5 David wrote, "I lay down and slept; I awoke, for the LORD sustains me." He wrote this psalm while fleeing from his son Absalom, who had formed an insurrection party to throw David off the throne of Israel. We cannot explain a peace that reigns in the midst of distressing circumstances.

In the same way, we cannot fully understand the peace of Peter in Acts 12. Herod had arrested both James and Peter. James was immediately beheaded, and Peter was thrown into prison until the end of Passover. The Scripture says, "On the very night when Herod was about to bring him forward, *Peter was sleeping between two soldiers*" (12:6). In Acts 16 Paul and Silas are beaten and thrown into prison. While in prison, they "were praying and singing hymns of praise to God, and the prisoners were listening to them" (16:25). This kind of peace truly passes understanding.

Third, real peace *guards* the heart and mind. The Greek word that is translated "guard" in Philippians 4:7 literally means, "to stand as a garrison." The same word is used in 2 Corinthians 11:32: "the ethnarch under Aretas the king was *guarding* the city of the Damascenes in order to seize me." Peace that guards the heart and mind is peace that stands as protection against an enemy. The enemy is named in Philippians 4:6, "Be anxious for nothing." Anxiety is the enemy against which God's peace, which is beyond understanding, guards our hearts and minds—the inner man.

Who can experience this peace? The fourth important aspect of this peace is its comprehensiveness. *All believers* can experience this peace. Philippians 4:7 is for all believers. Paul said that this peace is "in Christ Jesus." Anyone who is in Christ Jesus—who knows Him as Savior and Lord—can experience this peace in one's life. Anxiety can be defeated!

## APPLICATION

Thus far we have examined the seriousness of the problem of anxiety, and we have seen that it can be solved with God's peace. Before we close this chapter, I would like us to take some time to consider how great a problem we personally have with worry. I suspect that some of us are truly unaware of the extent of anxiety in our lives. We may not have ulcers, we may not call ourselves a worrywart, but I believe that anxiety is a sin that all believers struggle with to some extent.

From careful study of biblical statements regarding anxiety and from my experience with people as a biblical counselor, I have put together a checklist of worry symptoms. As you proceed through this list, evaluate each item carefully and honestly. You cannot address and solve the problem of anxiety until you know that you *have a problem*. As you read through the statements in this Worry Quotient Inventory, rate yourself using the scale provided.

## Worry Quotient Inventory

Rate yourself on these items, using the scale below:

4 = usually;   3 = often;   2 = sometimes;   1 = seldom;   0 = never

| | |
|---|---|
| 1. I become overexcited or react excessively. | 0   1   2   3   4 |
| 2. I have difficulty sleeping at night. | 0   1   2   3   4 |
| 3. I become easily confused and forgetful. | 0   1   2   3   4 |
| 4. I feel nervous and jittery. | 0   1   2   3   4 |
| 5. I feel pressured. | 0   1   2   3   4 |
| 6. I feel "out of it" or distant. | 0   1   2   3   4 |
| 7. I feel uncomfortable and ill at ease. | 0   1   2   3   4 |
| 8. I am dissatisfied. | 0   1   2   3   4 |
| 9. I find myself "racing the clock" to get things done. | 0   1   2   3   4 |
| 10. I get irritated. | 0   1   2   3   4 |
| 11. I have a sense of foreboding or gloom. | 0   1   2   3   4 |
| 12. I don't feel like doing anything. | 0   1   2   3   4 |
| 13. I feel (think) that I must be constantly busy or constantly working. | 0   1   2   3   4 |
| 14. I feel "down." | 0   1   2   3   4 |
| 15. I feel helpless, out of control. | 0   1   2   3   4 |

16. My stomach becomes upset. 0 1 2 3 4

17. My hands and face become moist from perspiration. 0 1 2 3 4

18. I feel my heart pounding. 0 1 2 3 4

19. I feel lightheaded. 0 1 2 3 4

20. My face becomes hot. 0 1 2 3 4

21. My fingers and hands shake. 0 1 2 3 4

22. I can't sit or stand still. 0 1 2 3 4

23. My muscles feel tense. 0 1 2 3 4

24. I have headaches. 0 1 2 3 4

25. My neck becomes stiff. 0 1 2 3 4

26. I am tired, fatigued. 0 1 2 3 4

27. I am critical of others. 0 1 2 3 4

28. I relive or rethink past negative experiences. 0 1 2 3 4

29. When I'm doing one thing, I am thinking about other things that I have to do. 0 1 2 3 4

30. I am so busy that I don't think that I have time for worship or devotions. 0 1 2 3 4

31. I anticipate failure. 0 1 2 3 4

32. I expect bad news. 0 1 2 3 4

33. I feel distant from God. 0 1 2 3 4

34. I am heavyhearted. 0 1 2 3 4

35. I wonder if God really cares. 0 1 2 3 4

36. When I make a mistake, I continue to think about it. 0 1 2 3 4

37. I have difficulty praising and thanking God. 0 1 2 3 4

38. I find it much easier to complain or find fault than to express appreciation. 0 1 2 3 4

39. I focus more on God's commands and warnings
    than on God's promises and encouragement to me
    in Christ.                                    0  1  2  3  4

40. I don't think I am appreciated or respected
    by others.                                    0  1  2  3  4

41. I foresee difficulties, problems, objections,
    calamities, "the worst."                      0  1  2  3  4

42. I prefer to avoid challenging situations rather than
    face them.                                    0  1  2  3  4

When you are finished, go back through the inventory
and note the items that you scored with a 2, 3, or 4. Items with
these ratings are often symptoms of worry. If you have a few
such scores, your problem with worry is probably moderate.
If you have many, your problem with worry is more advanced.

All of these items are possible signs of the existence of
anxiety in our lives. Just as a doctor considers the symptoms
of a disease to help identify that disease, it is important for us
to recognize the symptoms of anxiety in our lives so that we
know that this is a problem that we have to deal with. In the
next chapter we will consider the difference between legitimate
concern and sinful anxiety so that we can better identify our
own anxiety. We will also begin to learn about the solution to
this problem: what God has to say about dealing with anxiety.

1. In light of what you have just learned about yourself
   from this Worry Quotient Inventory, how much of a
   problem do you have with anxiety?

2. In light of what you have just learned about God's solution, peace, how often would you say that you experience

the peace of God in your life (always, often, sometimes, seldom, never)? (Never experiencing the peace of God may be an indication that you are not a true believer.)

3. In light of what you have learned about worry and peace, how (and in what ways) do you think God wants you to change? Since no one has fully attained God's peace, and never will until we reach heaven, there is room for change in every believer. Identifying the ways in which we need to improve is an important aspect of actually promoting improvement. Some people never improve because they never specifically identify how they need to change.

# 2

# LEGITIMATE CONCERN
# VERSUS SINFUL
# ANXIETY

Anxiety is an age-old problem, it is a common problem, and it is a serious problem. In the first chapter we discussed some of the reasons why anxiety is such a serious problem, and we looked at many different symptoms of the problem. In light of these many symptoms, it's unlikely that anyone can claim never to have struggled with the problem of worry. The Bible indicates, however, that anxiety is a problem, like all of man's problems, with a solution.

As believers, we do not have to be overcome by anxiety. When Jesus said in Matthew 6:25, "Do not be worried about your life," He was implying that it is indeed possible to not worry about our lives. When He said, "Do not let your heart be troubled," He implied that it is possible to not have a troubled heart. As we noted in the first chapter, Paul said, "Be anxious for nothing" (Phil. 4:6), and then went on to talk about the peace of God that passes understanding. The Scripture clearly teaches, then, that the problem of anxiety has a solution.

## GUIDELINES FOR OVERCOMING WORRY

In this chapter and the next, we are going to learn what that solution is. We are going to look at some biblical guidelines for addressing the problem of anxiety. The first thing that we will consider in combating the enemy of worry is that *we must be in a vital relationship with Jesus Christ.* In other words, we must know Christ as our personal Savior and Lord. That is the essential foundation for anything else that we may do to overcome this problem.

Jesus prefaced His teaching in Matthew 6:25 with these words: "For this reason I say to you. . . ." Who was the "you" to whom Jesus was referring? Looking back at Matthew 5:1–2, where Jesus begins His Sermon on the Mount, we find: "When Jesus . . . sat down, His disciples came to Him. He opened His mouth and began to teach them." Jesus was teaching His disciples, those who believed in Him, when He said, "Do not worry." Likewise, when He said, "Look at the birds of the air, that . . . your heavenly Father feeds them" (Matt. 6:26), He was speaking to people who were rightly related to God, who had become children of the heavenly Father.

Not everyone is a child of God. We become children of God by receiving Christ, as John 1:12 teaches. Although all people are indeed *creatures* of God, they are not all *children* of

God. Consider these words of Jesus: "Will He not much more clothe you? You of little faith!" (Matt. 6:30). Notice that Jesus did not say, "You of *no* faith." Only those without Christ have no faith at all. His listeners had faith, but their faith was small.

In John 16:33, when Jesus said, "These things I have spoken to *you*, so that in Me you may have peace," He was again speaking to His disciples. "In Me" is a phrase that means "in union with Me." Because His disciples were united to Him by faith, they could experience His peace. As we know, Paul made it very clear in Philippians 4:7 that the peace of God would "guard your hearts and your minds in Christ Jesus." This peace is possible only if we are vitally related to Jesus Christ.

When Christ paid the penalty for our sin with His death on the cross, He made it possible for us to be justified by faith. "Therefore, having been justified by faith, we have peace with God through our Lord Jesus Christ" (Rom. 5:1). Because of the work that Christ has done and continues to do in our lives, we can have peace. "For it is God who is at work in you, both to will and to work for His good pleasure" (Phil. 2:13).

The wonderful implication of this is that peace is not dependent on us. It does not matter what kind of personality we were born with or what kind of parents we had. "My peace I give to you," Jesus promised His disciples in John 14:27. This is not the peace of a sanguine personality or a happy home or an easy life. This is *God's peace*, the peace that surpasses all comprehension. Jesus Christ can give this peace to us regardless of our natural disposition or personality, regardless of our upbringing, and regardless of our present circumstances.

In Romans 15:13 Paul wrote to the church, "Now may the God of hope fill you with all joy and peace in believing."

Paul knew that it was possible for all believers to experience joy and peace in Christ, not because of what *we* are, but because of who *Christ* is. I am grieved when I hear, as I often do, believers who seem to think that they are victims of their personality, their childhood, or their present circumstances. They believe that they are doomed to a life of anxiety. Not so! True, it is not by our own power, but anyone can have peace by God's power.

Not only must we have a relationship with Christ, but that relationship must also be growing. This is a personal relationship that must develop and change throughout our lives. My relationship with my wife is a very personal relationship that has changed over time. We have developed emotional closeness in our marriage because we spend time together and because we are constantly working on our relationship. If either of us stops working, the relationship begins to deteriorate.

So also in our relationship with Christ—we must be willing to work at this relationship in order for it to grow. This requires effort on a daily basis. We need to be actively abiding in Christ, walking with Him and fellowshipping with Him. When a believer is close to Jesus, it is evident to those around because it shows in everything that one says and does. There is a discernible serenity in the life of a person who is walking closely with the Lord because God's peace is at work within. Therefore, the essential foundation for experiencing the peace of God is a vital, growing relationship with Christ.

## BE PREPARED FOR ACTION

The second biblical guideline for overcoming worry, and experiencing true peace, is that *we must be prepared for action by being informed.* In other words, we must carefully watch for certain things in our lives. In Luke 21:34 Jesus said, "Be on your guard, so that your hearts will not be weighted down with . . . the worries of life." First Peter 5:7–8 speaks of "casting all your anxiety on Him, because He cares for you. Be of sober spirit, be on the alert." It is important that we be vigilant, watching for danger, on the lookout for temptations to worry.

Of course to do this, we must know what we are looking for. We cannot spot the enemy of anxiety if we do not know what it looks like. For this purpose, we first need to be able to accurately identify and distinguish between legitimate concern and sinful anxiety. Jesus never condemned legitimate concern. He did condemn anxiety, however, and we must know the difference so that we can properly discern when concern becomes sin.

## WORRY DEFINED

Anxiety, or worry, is an abuse of a God-given emotional response. The Greek word for "worry" is *merimnaō*, but there are several places in the Scripture where this same word is used to describe legitimate concern. In Philippians 2:20 Paul said of Timothy, "For I have no one else of kindred spirit who will genuinely be *concerned* for your welfare." The word that is translated "concerned" is the Greek word *merimnaō.* Considering this use, it is apparent that *merimnaō* is *not* sinful anxiety. There is certainly a place for legitimate concern for others.

The problem arises when this legitimate concern is left unchecked or applied irresponsibly. The Greek word *merim-*

*naō* is used in Matthew 6:25–34 where Jesus condemns sinful concern about worldly things. It is also used in Mark 4:19 regarding the seed choked out by anxiety, in Luke 10:41 regarding a troubled Martha, and in Philippians 4:6 regarding the enemy of peace. How, then, do we properly distinguish between legitimate concern and sinful anxiety in the Scripture?

Look again at the passage in Matthew 6 regarding worry. In verse 26 Jesus said, "Look at the birds of the air, that they do not sow, nor reap nor gather into barns, and yet your heavenly Father feeds them." If we look at this verse superficially, we may think that Jesus was simply saying that birds are completely unconcerned about their food. After all, they don't plant and tend gardens; they don't store up food in a cellar. If we consider more carefully, though, we will see that the birds still have responsibility in providing themselves with food. God has given them wings to go out and find food. They cannot sit in their nests and wait for food to fall out of the sky; that would be an irresponsible lack of concern. Jesus was saying that while they work for their food, they also trust that God will make it available. They do not spend time worrying about whether they will find it or not.

God expects us to be responsible people. He expects us to make reasonable plans for the future and to make reasonable investments with our money. He expects us to be concerned about providing our family with food and clothing and other necessities. That is our responsibility as good stewards of what He has given us. In Luke 14:28 Jesus said, "For which one of you, when he wants to build a tower, does not first sit down and calculate the cost to see if he has enough to complete it?" Within the larger context of counting the cost of being a disciple, Jesus was teaching us to consider beforehand what we are going to do. That is legitimate concern.

## EUSTRESS VERSUS DISTRESS

The term *eustress* is sometimes used to describe the good, legitimate kind of care that the Bible does not condemn. The Greek prefix *eu* literally means *good*. For example, a *eulogy* is a speech of praise, often given at a funeral. In preparing the material for this book, I experienced *eustress*. I was legitimately concerned about presenting true and useful teaching that would edify my readers, and so I spent many hours in preparation. That was a good kind of stress.

There is a point, however, when good stress becomes bad stress, or "distress." This kind of concern is destructive and is what the Bible refers to as sinful anxiety or worry. In the first chapter we looked at many different symptoms of worry in our lives—evidences that we have a problem with anxiety. These can be helpful in pointing out to us areas of our lives in which we are struggling with anxiety. But how do we know when our legitimate concern crosses the line to sinful anxiety—when our care becomes worry? What defines worry?

These are important questions to answer rightly because many people get them wrong. Some people pass off their sinful worry by simply relabeling it as legitimate concern. Others simply relabel themselves; they are not worriers, they are "serious" people, or even "spiritual" people. Still others deny their anxiety completely, like the alcoholic who insists that he is just a social drinker. And some people just dismiss it as an unchangeable aspect of their temperament or consequence of their upbringing.

For our study, we will define "anxiety" as a sense of misgiving or uneasiness about what may happen to us or to someone or something that we care about. It is often connected with a sense of dread, dismay, and alarm. Anxiety is concern that has become a source of emotional torment. One way to know when the line between care and anxiety has been crossed is by paying attention to our natural, often physical, responses to distress.

## SYMPTOMS OF WORRY

For example, some people have a hard time sleeping when they are anxious. Some people bite their fingernails, experience stomach cramps, eat too much, or forget to eat at all. It is important for us to identify our own tendencies so that we can use these signals as warnings that we are succumbing to sinful worry. Some of these physical tendencies were listed in the Worry Quotient Inventory in chapter 1, but you may experience others. If our mind is alert, watchful for the signs, we can kill the seed of worry before it grows into serious anxiety.

Another way of discerning when the line has been crossed is by identifying sources of anxiety. All anxiety can be broken down into two large categories. The first category is anxiety that is caused by *primary* sources: deeply rooted sin issues in our lives. We will consider seven different primary sources of worry. The second category is anxiety that is caused by *sec-*

*ondary* sources: circumstances and people that we encounter on a daily basis. We will consider the latter category first.

## Secondary Sources of Worry

There are innumerable secondary sources of worry in this world, but we will look at just a few that are mentioned in Scripture. In Matthew 6:25 Jesus pointed out that we worry about our life. This includes anxiety about our health and our physical provisions (food, clothing, and such). Then, in Matthew 6:31, Jesus changed the pronoun to "we," and in so doing identified another source of worry: other people. We worry about our family and our friends, and their well-being.

In Matthew 6:32 Jesus pointed out yet another secondary source of worry. He said that we sometimes worry because other people are worrying. "For the Gentiles eagerly seek all these things." How often do we allow the prophets of doom on the television or in the newspaper to get us worried about something? We also worry about the future, as Jesus indicated in Matthew 6:34 when He cautioned us not to worry about tomorrow.

Jesus addressed the fact that we worry about being inadequate in Matthew 10:19: "But when they hand you over, do not worry about how or what you are to say; for it will be given you in that hour what you are to say." We worry that we will fail in a time of testing, that we will appear dumb, that we will be unable to defend ourselves. Later in that passage Jesus identified our worry about being physically hurt: "Do not fear those who kill the body but are unable to kill the soul" (Matt.

10:28). He went on to say that the Father cares for the sparrows, and we are worth much more than sparrows.

In the context of this passage in Matthew 10, we can also infer some other secondary causes of worry: being falsely accused, being overpowered, being taken advantage of, and being rejected and mistreated. Further, Jesus pointed out our tendency to worry about not being able to fulfill our responsibilities. In Luke 10:41 He said to Martha, "You are worried and bothered about so many things." In the context of this passage Jesus was also pointing out several related worries: being a failure, not being able to meet goals, the indifference of others to things we feel are important, the irresponsibility of others, and jealousy of others and their circumstances.

Jesus addressed the disciples' anxiety about the future, about their insecurity in their relationship to Him, and about what Christ thought about them in John 13 and 14. We all struggle with similar worries. There are many other sources of secondary worry mentioned in the Bible, but these are a sample of ones that I believe we can all easily identify with. It is essential for us to be able to identify these secondary sources of anxiety so that we can stop, ask for forgiveness, and then act to remove the sources of worry.

## PRIMARY SOURCES OF WORRY

There are other things that are *primary* causes of worry. These are things that are often deeply rooted in our lives and that underlie the secondary sources that we have just discussed. In Matthew 6:19–23 Jesus implied in His teaching that one of the primary causes of anxiety in our lives is an *incorrect value system.* In verses 19–20 He said, "Do not store up for yourselves treasures on earth, where moth and rust destroy, and where thieves break in and steal. But store up for yourselves treasures in heaven." In other words, when our minds are focused on temporal things, we can easily become anxious about the things that can affect and destroy them. For example, if we did not care so much about our car, we would not worry about its getting dented. If we were not so attached to our present lifestyle, we would not worry about the state of the economy. Misplaced values are a significant cause of much of our anxiety involving material things. This primary source of anxiety is closely connected to the next, because misplaced values are the result of trying to serve two masters.

Another primary source of anxiety that Jesus identified in this same passage is focusing on earthly treasure rather than on heavenly treasure. Or, as Jesus restated later, *trying to serve two masters.* In verse 24 He said, "You cannot serve God and wealth." Jesus made it clear with these words that it is not that we *should not* serve two masters, but that we *cannot* serve two masters. It is impossible; they both demand complete control of our lives. Either God is truly Lord of our lives, or man is the lord of our lives. Because God's values and man's values are in direct contrast to each other, no one can serve both at once.

This is perhaps the most significant primary source of anxiety for believers. We are not truly, totally committed to Christ. We attempt to hang on to as much of this world as we can while trying to serve God at the same time. We do not really believe that our joy will be complete and all things that we need will be given to us in Christ alone, and so we find ourselves torn in half as we try to keep one foot in the world and the other in the kingdom of God. As a result, our priorities get confused and out of order. When we experience anxiety, we need to stop and question ourselves: "Am I truly, practically, daily submitting to the Lordship of Jesus Christ?"

A third primary source of anxiety is *distorted thinking*. This is apparent in many of the things that Jesus said throughout Matthew 6:25–34. For example, "Do not be worried about . . . what you will eat. . . . Is not life more than food ?" (6:25). In other words, He was telling us to stop thinking illogically. We all know that life is more important than food or clothes, but sometimes we forget what we know or our thinking gets turned around.

"Look at the birds of the air, that they do not sow, nor reap nor gather into barns, and yet your heavenly Father feeds them. Are you not worth much more than they?" (6:26). Of course we are more important to God than birds, but we do not always think logically about these things. We see that God provides for His creatures, but we fail to make the connection that God will indeed provide for us as well—and much more so.

This is sometimes called "filtering." Objectively speaking, every circumstance of life has positive and negative aspects. Those who worry filter out the positive aspects and focus primarily on the negative aspects, often magnifying them as well. When we filter out what God promises and commands us, we end up looking only at the false, failed promises of the world. Distorted thinking also ties into incorrect values, which we looked at earlier. All of these things lead to anxiety.

A fourth primary source of anxiety is *self-ism*. Self-ism is a preoccupation with oneself. Jesus identified this primary source of worry in Matthew 6 when He talked about people whose only concern was their own needs: what they would eat, or drink, or wear (6:25). Self-ism has many manifestations, among them pride, perfectionism, and trying to do too much. We are preoccupied with and focused on ourselves because we think too highly of ourselves and we think too much of our accomplishments.

First Peter 5:5–7 identifies pride as a source of worry: "You younger men, likewise, be subject to your elders; and all of you clothe yourselves with humility toward one another. . . . Therefore humble yourselves under the mighty hand of God . . . casting all your anxiety on Him, because He cares for you." Peter pointed out the link between pride and anxiety in this passage by informing us that if we are humble, we will save ourselves from much anxiety. Why is this? It is because proud people want to control every situation and they experience anxiety when they cannot. Proud people think that whatever is not in their control is doomed to failure.

"Therefore humble yourselves under the mighty hand of God." Peter was commanding us to renounce our pride and submit to God. He was also reminding us that we are submitting to the *mighty* God: the only One who can really control any situation, the only One who can make anything come out right, and the only One who can effectively change a sinful heart. How we need to be reminded of this!

As a parent, I sometimes found myself becoming anxious for my children. I wanted them to turn out a certain way and I felt responsible for making that happen. Of course, they did not always cooperate with me and that sometimes caused me to worry. I was worried because of my pride—because I was trying to do God's work. Yes, as their father, I was responsible to teach them, to pray for them, to love them, and to provide for them. But, as Paul said, though I could plant and water, only God could make them grow (1 Cor. 3:7). To assume that I could do anything more was pride, and when pride took hold, it caused anxiety.

Perfectionism, another manifestation of self-ism, is also a source of anxiety. Who of us is ever perfect? When we focus on doing everything perfectly, we inevitably experience anxiety because we are aiming for something that is out of our reach. Perfectionism causes us to be inflexible, and anxiety comes when someone or something does not conform to our expectations. The greatest danger of perfectionism, however, is that it really is a denial of our need for redemption in Jesus Christ because a perfect person does not need salvation. None of us, of course, is perfect. We all need forgiveness and redemption in Christ.

A third manifestation of self-ism is trying to do too much, and this likewise leads to anxiety. In Luke 10:41 Jesus upbraided Martha that she was "worried and bothered by so many things." In other words, her plate was too full. As I think back over my life, my parents were two of the hardest-working people that I have known. My father was a farmer, and between the two of them, they worked day and night, day after day. From watching them and listening to them, I learned that one of the most important things in life was to be busy— all the time. When I wanted to please my parents, I got busy.

What I learned as a child, I carried into adulthood. As a new pastor, I got busy. I wanted the church members to think that I was a hardworking pastor, and so I filled my schedule with responsibilities. The problem was how well it worked. Those church members thought that I was so busy that they had better not bother me. I was unapproachable, unable to meet their needs, because I was so concerned with doing too many things. Again, this is a result of self-ism, and it causes anxiety because a person who is trying to do too many things becomes, like Martha, worried about getting them all done.

*A superficial approach to the Word of God* is the fifth primary source of anxiety. Jesus taught this in the parable of the four soils when He contrasted the thorny soil and the good soil: "And the one on whom the seed was sown among the thorns, this is the man who hears the word, and the worry of the world and the deceitfulness of wealth choke the word, and it becomes unfruitful. And the one on whom seed was sown on the good soil, this is the man who hears the word and understands it; who indeed bears fruit" (Matt. 13:22–23). The effect that the Word of God has on someone's life is directly related to the way in which one approaches it. Worriers do nothing with what they hear; but consider, by contrast, what the "good soil" person does.

First, the person whose heart is good soil *hears* the Word. In other words, he listens carefully. Second, this person *understands* the Word. After hearing it, such individuals think about it carefully, making sure that they know what it means. Third, they *accept* the Word. "And they hear the word and accept it and bear fruit" (Mark 4:20). When they have understood it properly, they receive the truth into their life. Fourth, these people *retain* the Word. They make every effort to hold on to what they have learned by memorizing it, meditating on it, writing it down, and reviewing it. The biblical truths that they learn in church or in their personal study stay with them throughout their day and from day to day. "These are the ones who have heard the word in an honest and good heart, and hold it fast" (Luke 8:15).

Finally, "good soil" people apply the Word in their life, "and bear fruit with perseverance" (Luke 8:15). Hearing, understanding, accepting, and retaining are not enough. In fact, all of these are in vain if the Word is not lived. The "good soil" person is one who obeys the Word and looks for practical ways to apply it in life. In so doing, the Word is able to bear fruit. On the other hand, the person whose life is thorny soil never gets past hearing the Word because the truth is quickly choked out by anxiety. Such people never understand, never accept, never retain, and, of course, never apply. Overcoming anxiety requires a proper approach to the Word of God.

*Laziness or irresponsibility* is the sixth primary cause of anxiety in our lives. In the parable of the ten talents Jesus condemned laziness. As believers, we have a responsibility to use the resources that we have been given to further the kingdom. The servant who failed to put to work the money entrusted to him was called wicked, lazy, and worthless (Matt. 25:26–30). How does laziness cause anxiety? We are tempted to worry when, as a result of not fulfilling our responsibilities in a timely fashion, we are faced with an overwhelming task and not enough time left to complete it.

For example, think of the student who leaves the final paper of the semester to the last week, or even day. By irresponsibly ignoring the approaching deadline, this person puts himself or herself in the position of having too much to do and not enough time to do it. He or she becomes anxious about the task, worrying that he or she will not be able to get it done in time and/or not be able to do it well. Indeed, much student anxiety regarding exams, projects, and papers is directly connected to the fact that they are unwilling to work ahead of time and then feel overwhelmed at the last minute.

Or, think of the person paying his bills at the end of the month, worrying about whether he will have enough money. Often, one can prevent that kind of anxiety by sticking to a responsible budget throughout the month. Laziness in bookkeeping or irresponsibility in spending puts us in the position of being tempted to worry about our finances. There are many other ways in which our laziness and irresponsibility become a source of anxiety. It is very important that we learn to recognize the underlying sin so that we can properly address both the sinful anxiety and its sinful cause.

### THE ULTIMATE CAUSE OF WORRY

Finally, a primary source of anxiety in our lives is *unbelief.* In other words, our faith is too small. In a way, all of the other primary sources we have discussed can be directly linked to this last one. In John 14:1 Jesus taught, "Do not let your heart be troubled; believe in God, believe also in Me." When we worry, it is really because we lack faith in God and His promises. We do not believe that He will provide for our needs as He promised. We do not believe that His grace is sufficient for us as He said. This lack of faith results in anxiety.

Understanding the primary and secondary causes of anxiety in our lives is an important step toward solving the problem. If we are really serious about overcoming worry, we need to be willing to search out its sources. This is all a part of being prepared to act against anxiety by being informed. In truth, anxiety is itself just a symptom of some disease—some sin—in our life. The anxiety is certainly sin, but it is caused by other sin. We must find out what this sin is so that we can repent of it and deal with it.

Serious problems require serious solutions. Since anxiety is a serious, many-faceted problem, we might expect that its solution would not be quick or simple. We have studied the first two biblical guidelines for addressing this serious problem of worry. A vital, growing relationship with Jesus Christ is the necessary foundation. Then, we must prepare ourselves for action by being informed about the difference between legitimate concern and sinful anxiety, and about the sources of worry in our lives. In the next chapter, we will consider the third biblical guideline for overcoming worry: strengthening and using our faith.

## APPLICATION

### Occasions of Worry Inventory

Use the following list to rate yourself concerning the things about which you are most prone to worry. In column 1, rate yourself on how often you worry about this item in question:

4 = usually,   3 = often,   2 = sometimes,   1 = seldom,   0 = never.

In column 2, rate the intensity of your worry about each of these items:

95–100% = could not be more intense;
60–94% = varying degrees of severe nervousness or uneasiness;
40–59% = moderately severe;
25–39% = moderate;
10–24% = slight;
5–9% = very slight;
0–4% = nonexistent or almost so.

| Occasion | How Often | How Severe |
|---|---|---|
| 1. Suffering physical injury | | |
| 2. Becoming ill | | |
| 3. Inexplicable aches, pains, internal feelings or thoughts | | |
| 4. Personal death or dying | | |
| 5. Death of others | | |
| 6. Not being able to take care of oneself | | |
| 7. Not being able to take care of others | | |
| 8. Being attacked or abused by others | | |
| 9. Becoming disabled | | |
| 10. Past failure(s) | | |
| 11. Present failure(s) | | |
| 12. Losing control of oneself (emotions, passions, words, actions, etc.) | | |

| Occasion | How Often | How Severe |
|---|---|---|
| 13. Being rejected by others | | |
| 14. Being dominated by others | | |
| 15. Doing foolish things | | |
| 16. Past traumatic events or experiences | | |
| 17. Being excluded | | |
| 18. Being disapproved | | |
| 19. What may happen in the future | | |
| 20. Being incompetent | | |
| 21. Evil thoughts | | |
| 22. Poor performance | | |
| 23. Repetitive mental images or thoughts | | |
| 24. Losing one's mind ("mental illness," insanity) | | |
| 25. Making a mistake | | |
| 26. Displaying a weakness or fault to others | | |
| 27. Not being able to fulfill one's responsibilities | | |
| 28. Not being as good, successful, appreciated, intelligent, or skilled as others | | |
| 29. Not achieving one's goals | | |
| 30. Past sin | | |
| 31. Present sin | | |

| Occasion | How Often | How Severe |
|---|---|---|
| 32. Relationship with God | | |
| 33. Being rejected by God | | |
| 34. Being punished by God | | |
| 35. Not achieving God's goals by one's own efforts | | |

## Primary Reasons for Worry Inventory

Use the following list to rate the extent to which the *primary sources for worry* cause you personal anxiety:

4 = usually,   3 = often,   2 = sometimes,   1 = seldom,   0 = never.

1. An incorrect value system, being too concerned about worldly values instead of God's values    4 3 2 1 0

2. Lack of total focus on and commitment to Christ (trying to serve two masters)    4 3 2 1 0

3. Filtered thinking—overlooking or ignoring positive aspects and being preoccupied with negative things    4 3 2 1 0

4. Wanting to be, and thinking I should be, in control of what only God can and should control    4 3 2 1 0

5. Perfectionism, legalism, a performance orientation to life, failure to think and live by grace    4 3 2 1 0

6. Taking on too many responsibilities, trying to do too much and not being able to handle all I have taken on    4 3 2 1 0

7. Laziness, failure to discipline myself to use my time wisely    4 3 2 1 0

8. Being feeling-oriented, doing what I feel like doing instead of what I should do; doing what is easiest and

|   | most appealing rather than doing what may be the hardest and most important | 4 | 3 | 2 | 1 | 0 |
|---|---|---|---|---|---|---|
| 9. | Procrastination | 4 | 3 | 2 | 1 | 0 |
| 10. | Wrong priorities | 4 | 3 | 2 | 1 | 0 |
| 11. | A superficial approach to God's Word, a failure to study, memorize, meditate on, and apply the truths of God's Word | 4 | 3 | 2 | 1 | 0 |
| 12. | Unbelief in God and His promises, a lack of practical trust that God is who the Bible says He is and will do (for me and others) what He says He will do | 4 | 3 | 2 | 1 | 0 |

# 3

## STRENGTHENING AND USING YOUR FAITH

Jay Adams told a story about a man named Joe who found a novel way of dealing with his worry problem. Joe was widely known to be a worrywart, but one day his friend Bill noticed that Joe was a changed man. When he asked what had happened, Joe replied that he had hired someone, at a thousand dollars a day, to do his worrying for him. Bill immediately asked him how he could afford it. Joe responded, "I can't. But that's not my problem because he does all the worrying for me!"

Joe solved his problem by paying someone else to carry his load. I suspect that there are many thousands of people who would like to do the same, were it possible. I believe, however, that even if it were possible for us to find someone to worry for us, we would still worry. We would find it nearly impossible to completely hand over our burden of anxiety.

Why should we carry a burden that someone else is willing to bear? This is an excellent question—one that many believers should spend more time thinking about—because, as believers, we all have Someone who is willing to carry our burdens! In Psalm 55:22 David counseled, "Cast your burden upon the LORD and He will sustain you; He will never allow the righteous to be shaken." Our Lord Jesus invited us to bring to Him our burdens: "Come to Me, all who are weary and heavy-laden, and I will give you rest" (Matt. 11:28). First Peter 5:7 urges us to "[cast] all your anxiety on Him, because He cares for you."

In spite of Christ's promise to take our burden, we hang on to our anxiety. We continue to worry. We find it easy to talk about giving our cares to Jesus, but very difficult to actually do. The fact that it is difficult, however, does not mean that it cannot be done. As we have studied and learned from the Scripture, worry is an old problem, a common problem, and a serious problem. Regardless of these truths, however, the Bible also makes it clear that it is a solvable problem. By the power of the Holy Spirit it is possible to overcome anxiety in our lives.

## PEACE IS ALWAYS POSSIBLE

In John 14:1 Jesus said, "Do not let your heart be troubled," and in Philippians 4:6 Paul said, "Be anxious for nothing." It is clear from these and other passages that there is never a circumstance or situation that requires or justifies worry. It is always possible in the midst of any trouble to experience the peace of God, which passes all understanding. In acknowledgment of this, we began in chapter 2 to look at what the biblical guidelines for overcoming anxiety are.

We learned first that the foundation for overcoming anxiety is a personal, vital relationship with Jesus Christ. This is essential because the peace that passes understanding is not from us; it is from God and can be ours only by His grace. The Holy Spirit gives us the power to experience this peace through Christ. We learned also that this peace is available to all believers, regardless of their natural tendencies, personalities, or circumstances.

We then studied the second biblical guideline for overcoming anxiety, the need to be prepared to act by being informed. We must know the difference between legitimate concern and sinful worry. We must know our personal symptoms of worry—the visible signs that we are falling into anxiety. And we must know how worry evidences itself in our own life and be watchful for the physical cues that our body provides.

We also must know the underlying causes of our anxiety. We looked at many examples of both primary and secondary sources of anxiety. Knowing these helps us to identify the sin that is causing our anxiety so that we can repent of it and deal with it in our lives. Once we have identified and repented of it, we then must seek the power of the Holy Spirit to help us live peacefully and righteously before God and before the world.

That brings us to the third biblical guideline for overcoming anxiety. In order to live peacefully and righteously, we have to *strengthen and use our faith.* The Scripture makes it very clear that one of the primary sources of worry in our lives is a lack of faith. As I said in chapter 2, in a sense it is *the* primary cause, because all the others can be traced back to it. If we had greater faith, we would not have incorrect values or divided loyalties or distorted thinking, we would not be preoccupied with ourselves, we would not superficially regard the Word, and we would not be lazy or irresponsible. These are all evidences that our faith is too small.

If it is true that unbelief is the primary sin causing anxiety, then one of the keys to overcoming anxiety must be to *increase our faith.* In Mark 4:35–41 Jesus and His disciples get into a boat and go out onto the Sea of Galilee. No doubt being tired from a long day, Jesus falls asleep in the back of the boat. When a violent storm breaks out that threatens to capsize the boat, they wake Him and rebuke him, "Teacher, do You not care that we are perishing?"

Several of Christ's disciples were experienced fishermen, quite accustomed to being in boats in all kinds of weather, but this storm was too much even for them. They woke up Jesus because they thought they were about to die and did not know what else to do. Jesus immediately got up and calmed the storm with a word. Then He said to His disciples, "Why are you afraid? How is it that you have no faith?" Jesus indicated that they were worried because of their unbelief, and He rebuked them for it.

This is the same point that Peter makes in 1 Peter 5:7–9. In verse 7 he says that we should cast all of our anxiety on Christ. In the next verse he warns us to be sober and alert, watchful for the devil's attempts to devour us with anxiety. Then, in verse 9, Peter gives us the key to overcoming anxiety: "But resist him, *firm in your faith.*" If we want to battle with the enemy of sinful worry, we must be armed with strong faith.

In Psalm 37, sometimes called the "Fretter's Psalm," David addressed the problem of anxiety. Three times he wrote, "Do not fret." Three times he also told us what we are to do instead of worrying and getting upset. "Trust in the LORD" (37:3). "Trust also in Him" (37:5). "Rest in the LORD and wait patiently for Him" (37:7). Again, greater faith is the antidote to anxiety.

In light of these teachings, when we find ourselves getting worried, we can know that it is because we are lacking in our faith. If we want to overcome our anxiety, we must increase our faith. Indeed, 1 John 5:4 says, "For whatever is born of God overcomes the world; and this is the victory that has overcome the world—our faith." Ephesians 6:16 teaches, "In addition to all, taking up the shield of faith with which you will be able to extinguish all the flaming arrows of the evil one." And Romans 15:13 promises, "Now may the God of hope fill you with all joy and peace in believing." In the Scripture, God's peace is directly connected to faith.

## HOW TO GET A FAITH LIFT

Since faith is the key to overcoming anxiety, how then do we increase it? How do we increase our dependence on

God in a practical way so that we experience worry less and less? There are four steps to increasing faith in our lives. First, we strengthen faith through worship and prayer. Paul taught this in Philippians 4:6–7: "Be anxious for nothing, but in everything by prayer and supplication with thanksgiving let your requests be known to God. And the peace of God, which surpasses all comprehension, will guard your hearts and your minds in Christ Jesus."

When we are tempted to worry, first we need to replace that worry with worship. The word that is translated "prayer" in verse 6 includes the idea of worship. In the Bible there are a number of words used to describe prayer, and this particular one is a broad term that refers to the whole aspect of worship and all that it involves, including prayer. Therefore, Paul is essentially saying, "Don't worry; worship!"

Why is worship an appropriate response to anxiety? When we worship God, we recognize and declare His worthiness. We think about and praise Him for His majesty, His glory, and His holiness. In truth, when we forget the worthiness of God, it is then that we lose faith and begin to experience anxiety. Consider the example of the prophet Isaiah, who worshipped God at a time in his life when, I believe, he was being tempted to anxiety.

Isaiah was a man who loved his God and loved his people, but he was distressed by the rampant sin, immorality, and idolatry that he saw around him. He sensed that God was righteously angry with the people for their sin and about to judge them. At this time, Uzziah was king of Judah, and according to the Scripture, "He did right in the sight of the LORD" (2 Chron. 26:4). As a result, the Lord blessed him during his reign and he became a powerful and wealthy king. Then, Uzziah sinned against the Lord. "But when he became strong, his heart was so proud that he acted corruptly" (26:16). God judged Uzziah's pride by afflicting him with leprosy, and Uzziah soon died.

When Uzziah died, Isaiah was grieved by the loss of his king and, I believe, anxious about the fate of his people. Isaiah went to the temple to worship, and when he did, he saw a vision of the Almighty God, high and lifted up (Isa. 6:1). He heard the angels singing, "Holy, Holy, Holy, is the LORD of hosts, the whole earth is full of His glory" (6:3). God graciously took Isaiah's eyes off himself and his troubles and put them where they belonged, on Him. As a result, Isaiah's faith was enlarged and he was able to change his focus from being worried to serving God: "Here am I. Send me!" (6:8).

We see a similar situation in Acts 4. At that time, the apostles were preaching the gospel in Jerusalem. This happened not too long after Christ had been crucified, meaning, of course, that many of the same people who had seen Christ crucified were hearing the gospel preached. This upset the religious leaders in Jerusalem because many people were believing in Christ. So the religious leaders summoned the apostles into their midst and "commanded them not to speak or teach at all in the name of Jesus" (Acts 4:18). Then, "when they had threatened them further, they let them go" (4:21).

Upon release, the apostles quickly gathered together with the rest of the believers. It seems reasonable to assume that many of the believers would have been tempted to worry about what had just happened. However, instead of allowing their hearts to be filled with anxiety, they turned their hearts to worship. "They lifted their voices to God with one accord and said, 'O Lord, it is You who made the heaven and the earth and the sea, and all that is in them'" (4:24). After they had prayed and worshipped God, "the place where they had gathered together was shaken, and they were all filled with the Holy Spirit and began to speak the word of God with boldness" (4:31). Truly, worship is an effective response to anxiety.

Psalm 46:10 admonishes, "Cease striving and know that I am God; I will be exalted among the nations, I will be exalted in the earth." If we want to overcome anxiety, we must learn to stand in awe of God. We must take time to be quiet, to meditate on God, to pray and worship, and to let our hearts be filled with the knowledge of His greatness and His glory. When we do this, there will be no room left for anxiety because our faith will be too large.

Throughout the book of Revelation, we are given many glimpses into heaven. One of the things repeatedly described in these glimpses is the constant worship that is taking place. God's people and all the creatures of heaven are continuously praising and worshipping Him. Someday the things of this earth—the work of evangelism, marriages, family relationships, providing for daily needs—will all come to an end, but we will never stop worshipping God.

Therefore, since worship is something that we will be doing in heaven for all eternity, how much more importance should we place on it now! Not only should worship be a regular practice of our lives as believers, but also in light of Paul's instructions, we ought to especially train ourselves to worship when we find ourselves being tempted by anxiety. When our focus is on the greatness of our God, the troubles of this world become very small.

Second, Paul called us to "supplication" (Phil. 4:6). This word speaks to the attitude with which we should be approaching God. Paul was instructing us to come to God with earnestness, with humility, and with a sense of our utter dependence on Him. Our attitude should be the same as that of the tax collector in Luke 18 who, with his head bowed, beat his chest in anguish and cried, "God, be merciful to me, the sinner!" (18:13). This man recognized that God did not owe him anything but wrath and punishment.

We noted in chapter 2 that one of the primary causes of anxiety is self-ism: being consumed with ourselves and our interests. This attitude leads to anxiety as circumstances show us that the world is in fact not revolving around us and not in our control. In order to overcome anxiety, that attitude of pride needs to be replaced with humility. We need to admit our absolute inadequacy and dependence on God. We need to admit our sin and our need for God's grace. That is an attitude of supplication.

Third, Paul said to give thanks: "but in everything by prayer and supplication with thanksgiving" (4:6). When we are worried, our minds are focused on the negative aspects of our circumstances. Paul instructed us to focus on the positive aspects instead. First Thessalonians 5:18 says, "In everything give thanks; for this is God's will for you in Christ Jesus." Ephesians 5:20 teaches us to be "always giving thanks for all things in the name of our Lord Jesus Christ." And Philippians 4:4 exclaims, "Rejoice in the Lord always; again I will say, rejoice!"

## Two Ways to Give Thanks

As believers, we have countless things to thank God for even when our circumstances are troubling. We have salvation that no one can take away from us (John 10:28–29). We have complete forgiveness in Christ for all our sins (Col. 2:13). We have been blessed with all spiritual blessings in Christ (Eph. 1:3). We have been given an inheritance and the Holy Spirit (Eph. 1:11–13). For all these things we can give thanks at all times.

There are also many things that we can be thankful for that address our anxiety more directly. We can be thankful for God's promise to strengthen us, help us, and uphold us (Isa. 41:10). We can be sure that no weapon formed against us will prosper (Isa. 54:17) because "If God is for us, who is against us?" (Rom. 8:31). We can trust that God will finish the good work that He began in us in Christ Jesus (Phil. 1:6). We can consider our trials all joy because God is producing endurance in us so that we may be perfect and complete (James 1:2–4). When tempted to worry, we need to stop and give thanks for all of these things.

As believers, we give thanks to God in two ways. In good, untroubled times, we often give thanks "by sight." In other words, we give thanks for the visible, tangible ways in which God has blessed us. The other way in which we give thanks is "by faith." In times of distressing circumstances, our thanksgiving will mostly be by faith. It is in these times of trouble that we need to deliberately focus our minds on God's promises for deliverance.

Certainly, it is easier to give thanks by sight. However, as we obey God by giving thanks *at all times*—even when it is difficult to see good things to be thankful for—God will strengthen our faith and fill us with His peace. Notice that Paul said, "*in everything* give thanks." Thanksgiving ought to be a habit. Worship and supplication ought also to be a habit. We must train ourselves to turn to God for help every day and in every situation.

Fourth, Paul instructed us to "let [our] requests be made known to God" (Phil. 4:6). As we turn our minds to worship and prayer, with an attitude of supplication and thanksgiving, we are then to ask God specifically for what we need. James 4:2 says, "You do not have because you do not ask." In Matthew 7:7 Jesus promised, "Ask, and it will be given to you; seek, and you will find; knock, and it will be opened to you." Then He said, "Or what man is there among you who, when his son asks for a loaf, will give him a stone? Or if he asks for a fish, he will not give him a snake, will he?" (7:9–10).

Jesus was teaching several things with these words, and one of them is that we can and should *be specific* about the things that we ask of God. Bread and fish are specific requests. However, when we ask, we must realize that everything we receive from God is by His grace. We deserve nothing and He owes us nothing. So when we are tempted to worry, we should cast that burden on God and ask Him for the specific help that we need at that particular time.

Truly, if these four things were the regular practice of our lives, there would be far less anxiety in our lives. Worship, supplication, thanksgiving in everything, and specific requests for help are an essential part of strengthening and increasing our faith. They are an antidote for worry because they take our focus off ourselves and our circumstances and place it on God, where it belongs.

The second way in which we can strengthen our faith for the purpose of overcoming anxiety is by *learning to think properly*. In other words, we must learn to put off incorrect teaching and ideas and put on the mind of Christ. "The mind set on the Spirit is life and peace" (Rom. 8:6). Jesus emphasized the importance of right thinking in Matthew 6. He challenged his listeners to revamp their thinking: "Do not be worried about your life. . . . Is not life more than food, and the body more than clothing?" (6:25). He wanted His disciples to understand that since God had given to them their very life (a far greater thing), He could be trusted to give them their food and clothing as well (a much lesser thing).

Paul used the same kind of logic in Romans 8:32: "He who did not spare His own Son, but delivered Him over for us all, how will He not also with Him freely give us all things?" In other words, if God has already given us His best—Jesus as payment for our sins—then why would He not give us everything else that He has promised us? As believers, we have trusted God for our salvation, for forgiveness of sins, and for a guarantee of eternity in heaven. Why then are we not willing to trust Him for our food and clothes and health and all these other things that are of infinitely less importance than our salvation?

When we worry, it is because we do not trust God with these lesser things. This is what Jesus was pointing out in Matthew 6:25. He supported his argument with several illustrations: the birds of the air and the flowers of the field. He was challenging His disciples to think logically about their needs so that they would not be tempted to worry. If God provides food for birds, "are you not worth much more than they?" (6:26). If God clothes the flowers, "will He not much more clothe you?" (6:30).

Throughout this passage Jesus is challenging us to think about who we are and what we have as believers. The incorrect ways of thinking—worrying about food and clothes and other things—are how unbelievers can be expected to think. "For the Gentiles eagerly seek all these things" (6:32). In this context "Gentile" refers to someone who is not a child of God. A Gentile is a person who, as an enemy of God, does not understand God's way and lives to fulfill his own passions and desires. It is logical that such a person will have anxiety, because he has no real security in life.

On the other hand, as believers, we have security in life. We are children of God! "For your heavenly Father knows that you need all these things" (6:32). Therefore, it is illogical for us to worry about our physical needs, for God has promised to provide them and is more than capable of doing it. In fact, He wants to do it. "[Cast] all your anxiety on Him, because He cares for you" (1 Peter 5:7). We need to learn to think rightly.

In Philippians 4 Paul likewise urges us to think rightly in order to overcome anxiety. He follows his exhortation to "be anxious for nothing" in verse 6 with these words: "Finally, brethren, whatever is true, whatever is honorable, whatever is right, whatever is pure, whatever is lovely, whatever is of good repute, if there is any excellence and if anything worthy of praise, dwell on these things" (4:8). In other words, do not let your mind dwell on your difficult circumstances, your weakness, or your ignorance. Rather, let it dwell on God's purposes, God's power, and God's wisdom.

Peter also taught us to think properly in order to combat the enemy of anxiety. In 1 Peter 5:7 he instructed us to cast our worries on God. Then he said, "Be of sober spirit, be on the alert. . . . But resist [the devil], firm in your faith, knowing . . ." (1 Peter 5:8–9). Peter made it clear that it is only by clear and correct thinking that we can strengthen our faith against anxiety. He went on, in verses 9–11, to tell us some specific things that we can think about.

First, Peter reminded us that other believers are experiencing similar temptations and difficult circumstances and are being victorious: "knowing that the same experiences of suffering are being accomplished by your brethren who are in the world" (5:9). We are not alone in our suffering. Paul said, "No temptation has overtaken you but such as is common to man" (1 Cor. 10:13). There are many others in this world who have faced the same temptations to worry. God has helped them and He will help us.

Second, Peter wanted us to think about the fact that there is an end in sight. He pointed out that the sufferings that we are experiencing are "in the world. After you have suffered for a little while, the God of all grace, who called you to His eternal glory . . ." (5:9–10). A time is coming when we will be free from suffering and anxiety. When we are tempted to worry, we must think about the fact that, although troubling things are bound to happen, they are going to come to an end. Jesus promised, "In the world you have tribulation, but take courage; I have overcome the world" (John 16:33). By His grace God has called us to spend eternity in glory with Him. We have hope because we have a guaranteed future of perfect peace.

Third, we are taught in these verses to remember that our "experiences of suffering are being accomplished." In other words, our difficulties have a purpose. Many times we cannot see the purposes of God in our circumstances, and that tempts us to worry. It is when God's ultimate good in difficult situations is hardest to see that we find it easiest to become anxious. It is then that we need to think and remind ourselves of what we know. "And we know that God causes all things to work together for good to those who love God, to those who are called according to His purpose" (Rom. 8:28).

Fourth, Peter wanted us to remember that God is a God of all grace. "After you have suffered for a little while, the God of all grace . . ." (1 Peter 5:10). God's grace is more than able to help us. Consider His words to Paul: "My grace is sufficient for you, for power is perfected in weakness" (2 Cor. 12:9). There is no situation in life in which God's grace will not be enough. When tempted to worry, we need to think about this truth.

Fifth, we are reminded that we are "in Christ." We can be sure of God's help because it is guaranteed through Christ. We are not worthy of God's grace or attention, but we are recipients of it because of Christ. "For as many as are the promises of God, in Him they are yes" (2 Cor. 1:20). We do not need to despair because of our sin and unworthiness before God. We do not need to doubt that God will want to help us in our time of need. We are united to Christ, and therefore we will never be denied or forsaken because God cannot deny or forsake Himself (2 Tim. 2:13).

Sixth, Peter wanted us to think about the fact that, if we are believers, God is personally working in our lives to make us more like Christ: "the God of all grace . . . will Himself perfect, confirm, strengthen and establish you" (1 Peter 5:10). God is personally involved in our lives, He knows all about us, and He has a personal interest in each one of us. He is going to personally see to it that several things are accomplished in us.

One, He is going to see to it that we are perfected: made thoroughly complete and fully equipped to accomplish all things that we were appointed to accomplish. Two, He is going to see to it that we are confirmed: unburdened of all our insecurity, totally dependent on God, and trusting in Him for all things. Three, He is going to see to it that we are strengthened and established: made capable of enduring and overcoming all difficulties because we can do all things through Him who gives us strength (Phil. 4:13).

Finally, Peter reminded us, "To Him be dominion forever and ever. Amen" (1 Peter 5:11). When we are tempted to worry, we need to think about the fact that God is sovereign. He is in control and has all power and all authority in heaven and on earth. Daniel 4:35 asserts, "But He does according to His will in the host of heaven and among the inhabitants of earth; and no one can ward off His hand or say to Him, 'What have You done?' " All these things that Peter commanded us to think about in 1 Peter 5:9–11 are truths that we need to focus our mind on at all times, but especially in times when we are tempted to worry.

In our battle against anxiety we need to strengthen our faith by worship and prayer and by thinking properly. We also need to strengthen our faith by *developing godly relationships with other believers*. Hebrews 3:12–13 warns, "Take care, brethren, that there not be in any one of you an evil, unbelieving heart that falls away from the living God. But encourage one another day after day, as long as it is still called 'Today,' so that none of you will be hardened by the deceitfulness of sin." As believers, we are responsible to encourage, admonish, pray for, and edify each other at all times.

Many other verses in Scripture support this idea. Hebrews 10:24–25 says, "And let us consider how to stimulate one another to love and good deeds, not forsaking our own assembling together, as is the habit of some, but encouraging one another; and all the more as you see the day drawing near." First Thessalonians 5:11 teaches, "Therefore encourage one another and build up one another, just as you also are doing." Verse 14 continues, "We urge you, brethren, admonish the unruly, *encourage the fainthearted, help the weak*, be patient with everyone."

It is vital that we do not isolate ourselves from other believers because one of the duties of all believers is to encourage and build up others. If we separate ourselves, we cut ourselves off from this help that God has planned for us in the body of believers. When we experience anxiety, we need to make sure that we surround ourselves with godly people who can encourage and admonish us. In other words, people who can lift our spirits but who also can rightly point out our sin in a loving manner.

Lastly, we need to fight against anxiety by *utilizing our faith*—putting it into practice. In Philippians 4:9 Paul urged, "The things you have learned and received and heard and seen in me, practice these things, and the God of peace will be with you." This is a very clear instruction and promise that Paul gives. If we want to know God's peace, we need to obey the things that we have been taught. We must make a concentrated, deliberate effort to practice them in our everyday life.

It is not enough to know that anxiety is a serious problem; we must be willing to address it. It is not enough to know about the solution—God's peace—we must seek after it. It is not enough to know what our symptoms of worry are; we must look for and acknowledge them. It is not enough to recognize the sin that causes our anxiety; we must repent of it. It is not enough to learn or even understand the biblical guidelines for overcoming anxiety; we must use them.

We have to work at our relationship with Jesus Christ. We have to prepare ourselves for action by being informed about the sources of worry. And we have to do the things that are necessary to strengthen and use our faith: turn our minds to worship and prayer, learn to think properly, develop relationships with godly people, and utilize our faith. We must *do* these things.

Hebrews 5:14 says, "But solid food is for the mature, who because of practice have their senses trained to discern good and evil." First Timothy 4:7 exhorts, "Discipline yourself for the purpose of godliness." Overcoming anxiety is not the battle of a day; it is the ongoing war of a lifetime. This war requires soldiers who have been trained for battle by the regular practice of obedience to God's commands. "Those who love Your law have great peace, and nothing causes them to stumble" (Ps. 119:165).

We have been given a promise that if we are faithful in training ourselves, we will experience the peace of God even on this earth. "And the peace of God, which surpasses all comprehension, will guard your hearts and your minds in Christ Jesus" (Phil. 4:7). We also have been given a promise for God's help in doing this. "For I am the LORD your God, who upholds your right hand, who says to you, 'Do not fear, I will help you' " (Isa. 41:13). May God help us to hear His Word regarding these things and put into practice His plans for overcoming anxiety. "Now may the Lord of peace Himself continually grant you peace in every circumstance. The Lord be with you all!" (2 Thess. 3:16).

## APPLICATION

1. Evaluate your faith-growing endeavors by using the following scale:

   4 = as good and biblical as possible;
   3 = usually meaningful, biblical, vital, and beneficial;
   2 = some room for improvement;
   1 = much room for improvement, very poor/hardly existent;
   0 = as bad as it could be, nonexistent.

   a. My worship and prayer life _____
   b. My thoughts, attitudes, meditations, and self-talk
      _____
   c. My relationships with other people _____
   d. Utilizing my faith; practicing God's Word in my daily life and thoughts _____

2. Identify what can be done to make the four factors in question 1 more dynamic in your life.

   a. *Worship and prayer.* How can you improve worship and prayer in your life? What should you do to promote this aspect of your life? What has been helpful to you in the past? What things have you observed others doing that seem beneficial to them?

   b. *Thoughts and attitudes.* How can you make your thought life conform to Philippians 4:8? What practical things can you do to eliminate unbiblical, unproductive self-talk and replace it with biblical self-talk? What should you do to promote this aspect of your life? What has been helpful to you in the past? What things have you observed others doing that seem beneficial to them?

   c. *Relationships.* How can you make your relationships with other people a dynamic, godly, constructive reality in your life? What should you do to promote this aspect of your life? What has been helpful to you in the past? What things have you observed others doing that seem beneficial to them?

   d. *Utilizing and practicing faith.* How can you utilize and practice your faith? What does it mean, in practical terms, to seek first the kingdom of God and His righteousness (Matt. 6:33)? How can you practically exercise your faith in the twenty-first century? What should you do to promote this aspect of your life? What has been helpful to you in the past? What things have you observed others doing that seem beneficial to them?

3. In the light of your reflections on questions 1 and 2, what changes will you make in your life to increase your faith?

4. Meditate on the statement that Jesus made about the foolishness of worrying in Matthew 6:32.

a. Why does this truth make worrying foolish?

b. What does it say about us and about our view of God if we continue to worry? How does our worry reflect on God?

c. What are some of the basic biblical needs of a child?

d. Are most fathers willing to meet those needs? Write down all the things that a good father does for his children.

e. Read and reflect on the following passages: Psalm 103:13–14; Matthew 7:7–11; 2 Corinthians 1:3; Ephesians 1:3; Hebrews 12:7–10; 1 Peter 1:3; Jude 1. Summarize what these passages say to you about our heavenly Father. What encouraging things are stated in these verses about our heavenly Father that point out the irrationality of anxiety?

f. Write down anything else that you know about God that should lessen your anxiety.

g. Write down all the ways that you can remember that God has been a good Father to you (be very specific).

h. What opinion would people get of your heavenly Father if they knew what you really thought and felt about Him?

i. How can you improve your devotional time, Bible study, and prayer life? In what ways can they be improved so that God is more real and vital to you?

5. Meditate on Philippians 4:8 and write out your own definition of each of the eight qualities that are listed there. After you have done this, make a list of specific things that would fit under each of the eight qualities.

For example, we are to think on things that are "true." What does the word "true" mean? The word "true" means that which is in accordance with facts, with reality. It means that which is accurate and real, in contrast to that which is unreal or false. How do I know what is real, what is accurate, what is in accordance with the facts? Primarily, I know that by looking at things through the lens of God's Word. Therefore, at least in part, thinking on things that are true involves thinking about situations, problems, people, life, God, myself, Jesus, etc., from God's perspective. What does God say about the circumstances of my life? See Psalm 37:23; Romans 8:28–29, 37–39; 1 Corinthians 10:13; Philippians 4:13, 19.

Complete your list of things that are true and then follow the same procedure with each of the other qualities. You may find that some things overlap, but that is fine. In the future, use this list as a guideline for what you should regularly think about to prevent worry or to overcome it when it arises. For a period of time, until thinking this way becomes a habit, it will be helpful for you to read aloud and meditate on this list several times a day. As you do, pray that God would make this activity a dynamic thought- and life-changing reality, not just a mechanical exercise.

6. To further buttress this biblical concept of thinking properly, study Isaiah 26:3; Romans 12:2; and 2 Corinthians 10:3–5. Summarize what each of these verses has to say about the importance of and the results of thinking properly.

7. Examine Psalm 77 as a case study illustrating the importance and impact of our thoughts.

   a. What two ways of thinking does this psalm present (compare vv. 2–10 with vv. 11–20)?

   b. What were Asaph's thoughts in verses 2–10? in verses 11–20? How do verses 11–20 illustrate Philippians 4:8?

c. How would you characterize Asaph's thoughts in verses 2–10? in verses 11–20? (Hint: in the first section, his thinking was circumstance-centered, and he viewed God through his circumstances; in the second section, his thinking was God-centered, and he viewed his circumstances through God.)

d. What was the result of such thinking in the first section (vv. 2–4, 10)? in the second section (vv. 13–20)?

e. How do you account for the change in his thinking (vv. 11–12)?

f. What does all of this mean to you?

8. Think of the most pressing, anxiety-producing issue in your life and consider how the principles taught in this chapter can be specifically applied to help you overcome anxiety and experience the peace of God. Be specific, concrete, and practical.

# Part 2

# SPIRITUAL
# BURNOUT

### REKINDLING

### THE FLAME

# 4

## A New Word for an Old Problem

In recent decades a new word has been added to our vocabulary. I have heard this word used to describe the experience of certain pastors and church leaders. I have heard it used to describe the experience of both Christians and non-Christians, men and women, young and old, educated and uneducated. Every now and then, I see a new book or a conference advertised that promises to address this problem and help people to avoid it.

### Burnout Defined

What is this word? It is "burnout." Burnout refers to what is often a devastating experience involving feelings of blahness, indifference, apathy, boredom, confusion, tiredness, and loss of motivation—in some cases, virtual paralysis. It means that a person has reached a point of mental, emotional, physical, and spiritual fatigue. Sadly, it is even used as an excuse for the irresponsible actions of those experiencing it: spouses in their marriages, church members in the body of Christ, parents in their families, or employees in their workplaces.

While the word "burnout" may be new, the problem it describes is not. Burnout has been a part of human experience for a long time. We know this because the Bible frequently exhorts us not to succumb to burnout. Scripture never actually uses the word "burnout," but it does clearly describe the experience by using other words. For example, in 2 Corinthians 4 Paul warned believers not to "lose heart." When individuals lose heart, they experience what we commonly call "burnout" today: they lack enthusiasm, the zest for life, and excitement about life; they complain of being exhausted, perplexed, and dispirited. They are dissatisfied and joyless. They feel overwhelmed and paralyzed by their inadequacy and are unable to be as active and involved as they once were.

This problem is addressed in other places in Scripture as well, sometimes with the words "lose heart," and sometimes with the word "weary" or "faint." In Galatians 6:9 Paul said, "Let us not lose heart in doing good, for in due time we will reap if we do not grow weary." In Ephesians 3:13 he taught, "Therefore I ask you not to lose heart at my tribulations on your behalf, for they are your glory." And in 2 Thessalonians 3:13 he exhorted, "But as for you, brethren, do not grow weary of doing good."

## Burnout as a Common Experience: Biblical Examples

The Bible addresses this problem because God knows that we struggle with it, and He knows that it is a common struggle even among believers. Paul addressed the issue several times, but Jesus also encouraged His disciples not to lose heart (Luke 18). In the Old Testament, we know that people experienced burnout, or the temptation to burn out, because of what the psalmists expressed in some of their writings. In fact, the experience of burnout is frequently mentioned in the Psalms.

For example, David wrote in Psalm 6:6, "I am weary with my sighing; every night I make my bed swim, I dissolve my couch with my tears." Psalm 42:5 laments, "Why are you in despair, O my soul? And why have you become disturbed within me?" In Psalm 69:1–3 David used metaphors to more effectively describe his deep distress: "Save me, O God, for the waters have threatened my life. I have sunk in deep mire, and there is no foothold; I have come into deep waters, and a flood overflows me. I am weary with my crying; my throat is parched; my eyes fail while I wait for my God."

A similar experience is described in Psalm 73:2, 13–14: "But as for me, my feet came close to stumbling, my steps had almost slipped. . . . Surely in vain I have kept my heart pure and washed my hands in innocence; for I have been stricken all day long and chastened every morning." The writer of this psalm is saying that he is close to giving up on godliness, on obedience, on honoring God, because it does not seem to result in any good. He feels that even in his pursuit of holiness, he is being constantly punished. He is experiencing burnout.

Job certainly experienced burnout. Consider his words in Job 10:1–3: "I loathe my own life; I will give full vent to my complaint; I will speak in the bitterness of my soul. I will say to God, 'Do not condemn me; let me know why You contend with me. Is it right for You indeed to oppress, to reject the labor of Your hands, and to look favorably on the schemes of the wicked?' "

Job was feeling rejected by God, dissatisfied, discouraged, dejected, and generally miserable. Later he cried, "My spirit is broken, my days are extinguished, the grave is ready for me" (Job 17:1). Job was literally ready and willing to die. He continued this theme in Job 30:16–23:

> And now my soul is poured out within me;
> Days of affliction have seized me.
> At night it pierces my bones within me,
> And my gnawing pains take no rest.
> By a great force my garment is distorted;
> It binds me about as the collar of my coat.
> He has cast me into the mire,
> And I have become like dust and ashes.
> I cry out to You for help, but You do not answer me;
> I stand up, and You turn Your attention against me.
> You have become cruel to me;
> With the might of Your hand You persecute me.
> You lift me up to the wind and cause me to ride;
> And You dissolve me in a storm.
> For I know that You will bring me to death
> And to the house of meeting for all living.

Job was definitely experiencing the pain, confusion, distress, and misery of spiritual burnout.

The prophet Elijah experienced burnout as well. Though this man was a great prophet of the Lord, he came to a point in his life where he lost heart. In 1 Kings 19:4 Elijah pleaded with God, "It is enough; now, O LORD, take my life, for I am not better than my fathers." Again, in verses 10 and 14, he complained, "I have been very zealous for the LORD, the God of hosts; for the sons of Israel have forsaken Your covenant, torn down Your altars and killed Your prophets with the sword. And I alone am left; and they seek my life, to take it away."

Even Moses, the leader of the Israelites, was tempted to lose heart. In Exodus 32:30–32 Moses pleaded with God to forgive the sins of the people: "But now, if You will, forgive their sin—and if not, please blot me out from Your book which You have written!" Moses was ready to die because he was so utterly discouraged with the sins of the Israelites and the difficulty of being their leader.

Later, in Numbers 11, Moses lost heart again:

Now Moses heard the people weeping throughout their families . . . and Moses was displeased. So Moses said to the LORD, "Why have You been so hard on Your servant? And why have I not found favor in Your sight, that You have laid the burden of all this people on me? . . . I alone am not able to carry all this people, because it is too burdensome for me. So if You are going to deal thus with me, please kill me at once, if I have found favor in Your sight, and do not let me see my wretchedness." (Num. 11:10–15)

Moses again asked for death rather than the continuing burden of leadership because he was experiencing spiritual burnout.

NEW TESTAMENT EXAMPLES OF BURNOUT

Burnout occurred in New Testament times as well. In fact, the book of Hebrews was written to encourage believers who were greatly discouraged and ready to give up on their new faith. In Hebrews 3:6 we find this encouragement to maintain faithfulness: "But Christ was faithful as a Son over His house—whose house we are, if we hold fast our confidence and the boast of our hope firm until the end." It is followed by this warning:

"Therefore, just as the Holy Spirit says, 'Today if you hear His voice, do not harden your hearts as when they provoked Me, as in the day of trial in the wilderness. . . . Therefore I was angry with this generation, and said, "They always go astray in their heart, and they did not know My ways"; as I swore in My wrath, "They shall not enter My rest"'" (Heb. 3:7–11).

Then, a challenge is given to not lose heart and disobey God: "Take care, brethren, that there not be in any one of you an evil, unbelieving heart that falls away from the living God. But encourage one another day after day, as long as it is still called 'Today,' so that none of you will be hardened by the deceitfulness of sin. For we have become partakers of Christ, if we hold fast the beginning of our assurance firm until the end" (Heb. 3:12–14).

92 | SPIRITUAL BURNOUT: *Rekindling the Flame*

These exhortations to be diligent and to not lose heart continue in the next several chapters. Hebrews 6:11–12 says, "And we desire that each one of you show the same diligence so as to realize the full assurance of hope until the end, so that you will not be sluggish, but imitators of those who through faith and patience inherit the promises." Hebrews 10:23 encourages us with these words: "Let us hold fast the confession of our hope without wavering, for He who promised is faithful." And again in verses 35–36, "Therefore, do not throw away your confidence, which has a great reward. For you have need of endurance, so that when you have done the will of God, you may receive what was promised."

Why does the Bible have so much to say about burnout? Why are we repeatedly exhorted to not lose heart, to be diligent, to have endurance, and to continue on in faith? It is because God knows that burnout is a common experience and one that almost all believers will be tempted to give in to at some point. A quick Internet search revealed the universal nature of burnout in today's world. I found 518 articles on the subject addressing all aspects of the problem, including recognizing signs, prevention, recovery, and on and on.

Sadly, burnout seems to be almost as common among believers as it is among unbelievers. There are many people in churches today who, while claiming to be Christians, are burned out. They are joyless, apathetic, disengaged, unenthusiastic about their faith, and overwhelmed. They are uninvolved in ministry, they do not long to hear the Word of God preached, and they do not practice their faith on a daily basis. In the words of the apostle Paul, they have "lost heart."

Burnout is not only very common, but also very serious because of its detrimental effects on lives and ministries. Among other things, when people lose heart, they lose some very significant spiritual blessings. Consider the words of Isaiah 40:31: "Yet those who wait for the LORD will gain new strength; they will mount up with wings like eagles, they will run and not get tired, they will walk and not become weary." "Weary" is the translation of the Hebrew word for "losing heart." This verse, by stating what people who do not lose heart are blessed with, reveals three assets that those who are burned out lose: *strength, endurance, and enthusiasm.*

First, people who are burned out no longer experience "new strength" to face their challenges. Their hearts are not renewed and restored on a daily basis, as David's was when he wrote, "The LORD is my shepherd. . . . He restores my soul" (Ps. 23:1–3), and "On the day I called, You answered me; You made me bold with strength in my soul" (Ps. 138:3). A lack of spiritual strength affects a person in both soul and body; one loses spiritual and physical strength.

Second, people who are burned out no longer "mount up" like eagles or even "walk" anymore. They have lost their endurance. Eagles have a tremendous wingspan and can fly easily for long distances over any terrain—mountains, forests, valleys, and deserts. People who have lost heart cannot deal with the challenges and difficulties of life. They cannot persevere for long periods of time through all kinds of circumstances. In fact, they cannot even make steady progress—walk—because they have lost their ability to endure.

Third, people who have lost heart can no longer "run and not get tired." In other words, they have lost their enthusiasm for the things of the Lord. In Psalm 42 David lamented, "My tears have been my food day and night. . . . These things I remember and I pour out my soul within me. For I used to go along with the throng and lead them in procession to the house of God, with the voice of joy and thanksgiving, a multitude keeping festival" (42:3–4). A person who loses heart loses joy in the Lord and in the things of the Lord.

Losing strength, endurance, and enthusiasm are serious matters, but there are other serious consequences to burnout as well. In Ephesians 3:13 Paul said, "Therefore I ask you not to lose heart at my tribulations on your behalf, for they are your glory." The surrounding passage in Ephesians 3 reveals four more spiritual blessings that people who are burned out lose: eternal perspective, a sense of Christ's presence in their hearts, the fullness of God in their hearts, and a biblical view of God.

The first twelve verses of this chapter are an exhortation by Paul to his readers to not *lose their eternal perspective on their labors.* He reminds the Ephesians what a great privilege he had to be a minister of the gospel: "To me, the very least of all saints, this grace was given, to preach to the Gentiles the unfathomable riches of Christ" (Eph. 3:8). Very often, when believers become burned out, they forget what a privilege it is to serve God and to be His witnesses among men. Their ministry lacks passion and conviction because they no longer see it as eternally significant. Their focus shifts to their temporary weariness rather than remaining on the all-important task to which they have been called in Christ.

Paul recognized the serious consequences of losing heart, and he wrote to these believers to encourage them. After exhorting them to not lose heart in verse 13, he continued in verses 14–16: "For this reason I bow my knees before the Father, from whom every family in heaven and on earth derives its name, that He would grant you, according to the riches of His glory, to be strengthened with power through His Spirit in the inner man." Paul prayed that they would be given strength with power through the Holy Spirit so that they would not lose heart.

He went on in verses 17–19: "so that Christ may dwell in your hearts through faith; and that you, being rooted and grounded in love, may be able to comprehend with all the saints . . . the love of Christ which surpasses knowledge." People who lose heart also *lose a sense of Christ's presence in their hearts.* Paul prayed that this would not happen to these believers. He wanted them to continually know the unfathomable love of Christ, to be rooted and grounded in love.

Further, people who are burned out *lose the fullness of God in their hearts:* "that you may be filled up to all the fullness of God" (Eph. 3:19). In other words, they are not experiencing everything that God has for them—God's peace, joy, love, goodness, and faithfulness. God desires to fill us up with all these spiritual blessings in Christ, but we lose these blessings when we lose heart.

Finally, people who are burned out *lose a biblical view of God.* They no longer think about God as Paul described in verse 20: "Now to Him who is able to do far more abundantly beyond all that we ask or think, according to the power that works within us." People who have lost heart have a very diminished view of God. They see God as unconcerned, unwilling, and even unable to help them.

These are all serious consequences of a common but serious problem. Indeed, Christians experiencing burnout are, at best, ineffective and, at worst, destructive to Christian ministry, other people, and themselves. Losing these spiritual blessings, however, is not the only consequence of burnout. In the next chapter, we will consider additional consequences of losing heart: things that burned-out people start doing that they should not and things that they stop doing that they should be doing.

Before going on, consider your own heart and life. Are you experiencing the loss of any of the spiritual blessings that we have studied in this chapter? If so, it may be an indication that you are experiencing burnout to some degree. Be honest in evaluating yourself and pray that your heart would be open and willing to admit your struggle. Be encouraged as well because God has an answer to this problem. In chapters 6 and 7, we will consider both how to recover from spiritual burnout and how to prevent burning out in the first place (i.e., how to rekindle and maintain the flame of devotion to and enthusiasm for Christ).

> Now to Him who is able to keep you from stumbling, and to make you stand in the presence of His glory blameless with great joy, to the only God our Savior, through Jesus Christ our Lord, be glory, majesty, dominion and authority, before all time and now and forever. Amen. (Jude 24–25)

# APPLICATION

1. What is someone who is "burned out" experiencing?

2. What are the primary words that are used in our English Bible to describe this experience? (Identify the references where these words are used.)

3. Identify several Old Testament biblical characters who experienced spiritual burnout.

4. In each case, how did the burnout experience manifest itself? List specific ways in which the burnout was described.

5. Identify the primary New Testament examples of burnout discussed in this chapter.

6. How did each burnout experience manifest itself? List specific ways in which the Bible describes the burnout experiences of these people.

7. What spiritual blessings do people lose when they experience spiritual burnout?

8. Have you ever thought and felt the way the biblical characters in this chapter thought and felt? Describe what was going on in your life at the time. Describe specifically what you were thinking and feeling. Identify how your spiritual burnout affected you. Try to identify the reasons why you experienced this period of spiritual burnout.

9. Write out Isaiah 40:31 and memorize it.

# 5

## THE BAD NEWS
## ABOUT BURNOUT

In my experience as a biblical counselor, I have worked with many people who have described themselves as feeling overwhelmed, inadequate, and unmotivated. They say, "I feel disengaged and out of touch with reality. I feel like I'm removed from myself, just kind of floating around." These people are describing the experience commonly known as burnout, which Scripture refers to as losing heart or growing weary. In the previous chapter we discussed the nature of this problem and how common it is.

### MORE ABOUT THE EFFECTS OF BURNOUT

We began, at the end of chapter 4, to consider the seriousness of this problem by looking at two passages, Isaiah 40 and Ephesians 3. These passages list some of the spiritual blessings that are lost by people experiencing burnout. In this chapter, we will consider additional consequences of losing heart: things that burned-out people *start* doing as a result of their struggle and things that they *stop* doing when they have lost heart.

In Luke 18 Jesus told a parable to encourage His followers not to lose heart. This parable was on the subject of prayer because Jesus knew that people who lose heart *struggle with prayer.* Some simply stop praying altogether, thinking that prayer is a pointless exercise since God does not seem to hear or answer. Others continue to pray, but only in a half-hearted way, not expecting any kind of response or result.

Jesus' parable in Luke 18 tells the story of a persistent widow and a stubborn judge. The widow repeatedly pleaded with the judge for protection from an oppressor. After refusing many times, eventually the judge conceded—not because he cared about justice, but simply to make her go away. Jesus concluded the parable with these words: "Will not God bring about justice for His elect who cry to Him day and night, and will He delay long over them? I tell you that He will bring about justice for them quickly. However, when the Son of Man comes, will He find faith on the earth?" (18:7–8).

What kind of faith was Jesus referring to here? He was talking about faith that believes that God hears and answers prayer. When people lose heart, it is very difficult for them to maintain that kind of faith. People who are burned out no longer pray with conviction that God hears them. They no longer pray with expectation of being answered. If they pray at all, it is empty, obligatory prayer at best. The Scripture makes it clear that prayer should be at the center of every believer's life, and thus anything that interferes with prayer, such as losing heart, is a serious matter.

In this parable, Jesus made a lesser to greater argument for the purpose of encouraging His listeners to maintain faith. He pointed out that if an unrighteous judge would grant a widow's request simply because of her persistence, how much more will our heavenly Father, who *wants to give us good things*, listen to and answer our prayers! People who have lost heart, however, struggle with prayer.

## THINGS BURNED-OUT PEOPLE START DOING

In 2 Corinthians 4 Paul revealed four more things that a person who has lost heart will start doing: "Therefore, since we have this ministry, as we received mercy, we do not lose heart, *but* we have renounced the things hidden because of shame, not walking in craftiness or adulterating the word of God, but by the manifestation of truth commending ourselves to every man's conscience in the sight of God" (2 Cor. 4:1–2). The word "but" in this passage indicates a contrast between what people who have not lost heart and those who have lost heart will do.

First, Paul said that those who lose heart *start to approve and accept shameful things*. In other words, they start to practice sinful things that they know are wrong and wish to conceal from others. They no longer condemn sinful, shameful practices as they did before. They are like the people that Paul spoke of in Romans 1:32: "Although they know the ordinance of God, that those who practice such things are worthy of death, they not only do the same, but also give hearty approval to those who practice them." Philippians 3:19 says much the same when it refers to people "whose god is their appetite, and whose glory is in their shame, who set their minds on earthly things." These are people who glory in—enjoy—shameful things. They have lowered their standards and started to excuse behavior that they once knew to be sinful.

Second, people who have lost heart *start walking in craftiness* (2 Cor. 4:2). What does Paul mean by "craftiness"? This same word is used in several other places in Scripture: first, in Genesis 3:1 where the Word of God says that Satan deceived Eve by his craftiness, or subtlety and cleverness. In Ephesians 4:14 this word is used to describe how immature Christians can be easily turned aside from godliness: "As a result, we are no longer to be children, tossed here and there by waves and carried about by every wind of doctrine, by the trickery of men, by craftiness in deceitful scheming."

Again, in Luke 20:19–23 this word is used to describe the Pharisees' attempt to trick Jesus by pretending to be righteous and sincere in their questions when really they were attempting to draw Him into making a statement that they could use against Him before the Roman authorities. Jesus, of course, "detected their trickery" and answered them accordingly (Luke 20:23).

In the same way, those who have lost heart often become crafty. They may pretend to be what they are not, they may lie and deceive, and they may be selfish in all their thinking. They sometimes become dishonest about what is going on in their lives, about their motives, and about their spiritual needs.

To some extent, they may even deceive themselves about what they want and what they are capable of doing.

I once worked with a man who was a licensed psychologist, a university professor, and a declared atheist. By God's grace, he came to a saving knowledge of Christ while on a trip to Europe, and his life was completely turned around. Though he had questioned the validity of secular psychology even before becoming a Christian, he was convinced of the supremacy of God's Word in healing lives after he met Jesus.

We worked together in a counseling center. One day, as I walked down the hallway, I heard him say to someone in his office, "Show me the blood! Show me the blood!" When I asked him about it later, he explained that he had been counseling someone who repeatedly claimed to want to change, but did not. My colleague was using Hebrews 12:4, "You have not yet resisted to the point of shedding blood in your striving against sin." He challenged his counselee that though he claimed to want to change, he was not serious. If he were serious, he would both desire to change and be willing to do whatever it took to bring about that change—even to the point of personal pain and sacrifice.

In the previous verse, Hebrews 12:3, the writer says, "For consider Him who has endured such hostility by sinners against Himself, so that you will not grow weary and lose heart." People who have lost heart, who are burned out, are not willing to resist sin sacrificially. They claim to desire holiness, but they are deceitful and crafty in their lives. They deceive themselves, and they seek to deceive others because they are not willing to face the truth of their sin.

Third, Paul pointed out that people who have lost heart often *start to adulterate the Word of God* (2 Cor. 4:2). To adulterate something means to weaken and corrupt it by introducing impurities. In other words, burned-out people sometimes want the Bible *plus* something else. They weaken the Word of God by adding to it their own opinions and the opinions of others. Sometimes they seek to diminish its relevancy by pointing out its age, or they seek to diminish its supremacy by misinterpreting and distorting its message.

They may also adulterate the Word in their lives by avoiding what bothers them. They would rather not hear good preaching and teaching. When they do hear it, they excuse themselves from its message and from conviction by convincing themselves that it does not apply to them or their situation. They treat the Bible like a buffet line, reading and listening to what appeals to them and ignoring the rest as irrelevant to their life.

In contrast, Paul says that he and his fellow ministers of the gospel are "by the manifestation of truth commending ourselves to every man's conscience in the sight of God" (2 Cor. 4:2). In other words, because he held fast to the truth of God's Word and did not attempt to conform it or distort it to his own or anyone else's desires, Paul did not lose heart. People who lose heart are susceptible to changing the truth, and even turning to lies, to satisfy their sinful desires.

They may become like the people that Paul described in 2 Timothy 4:3–4: "For the time will come when they will not endure sound doctrine; but wanting to have their ears tickled, they will accumulate for themselves teachers in accordance to their own desires, and will turn away their ears from the truth and will turn aside to myths." These are people who live only to fulfill their own desires. They are "disobedient, deceived, enslaved to various lusts and pleasures" (Titus 3:3).

## THE FOCUS OF BURNED-OUT PEOPLE

This brings us to the fourth point that Paul made regarding people who have lost heart: they *start focusing solely on their own desires, rather than God's desires.* They are willing to do things that they feel they have to, like getting up for work every morning, paying taxes, and performing other unpleasant but necessary tasks, but they are not willing to do necessary spiritual things. They fail to pray, read the Bible, or go to church because they say they have no desire for these things. In truth, they fail to obey because they *do not desire to obey.*

God calls us to obedience whether we like it or not. Sometimes it is only the force of our will that gets us on our knees or into the Word of God, but that is obedience. When we excuse ourselves from the things of the Lord because we do not feel a desire for them, we are making a god out of the lusts of our flesh. Paul said that people will search out for themselves pastors and teachers who will tell them the things that they *want* to hear so that they will not have to listen to what they *ought* to hear.

One day, we will all stand before the judgment seat of God, and at that point it will no longer matter what we liked or disliked. It will no longer matter what we did on this earth for ourselves. Ecclesiastes 8:10 says, "So then, I have seen the wicked buried, those who used to go in and out from the holy place, and they are soon forgotten in the city where they did thus." Solomon is saying in this verse that the deeds of people who care only about man's approval—who go to church to be seen by people—will be forgotten as soon as they die.

How often do we think about the fact that whatever our reputation is among men, it will be soon forgotten when we die? It is foolish to live for the praise of men, and it is also foolish to think that we can get away with sin that is not punished on this earth, as the next verse teaches: "Because the sentence against an evil deed is not executed quickly, therefore the hearts of the sons of men among them are given fully to do evil." Though people may not face the consequences of their sins on earth, they will surely face them in the hereafter.

In 2 Corinthians 2:17 Paul said, "For we are not like many, peddling the word of God, but as from sincerity, but as from God, we speak in Christ in the sight of God." Paul knew that his life was always fully in God's sight, and he lived accordingly. So too is the life of every person; God knows our hearts. We may be able to fool men while we are alive, but we can never fool God. Thus, our main concern ought to be what God desires of us.

Paul said that because he was always in the sight of God and because he was united to Christ, he would not "peddle" the Word of God. A peddler is someone who wheels and deals to sell his wares. He lowers his price and throws in extras and generally does anything he possibly can to draw in a buyer. In the same way, someone who peddles the Word of God cuts corners from the truth, waters down the truth, and adds to the truth to make it more acceptable to listeners. He is more concerned about being accepted and having his message accepted than about speaking the truth at any cost. Being consumed by personal desires and lusts, ignoring the truth of God's Word, is a dangerous consequence of losing heart.

## Things Burned-Out People Stop Doing

In 2 Corinthians 4 we also learn some things that people *stop* doing when they lose heart. For one, people who lose heart *stop believing God's Word.* "But having the same spirit of faith, according to what is written, 'I believed, therefore I spoke,' we also believe, therefore we also speak" (2 Cor. 4:13). They begin to question the truth of God's Word, and as a result, they also *stop preaching Christ boldly and stop living as His servants.* In verse 5 Paul said, "For we do not preach ourselves but Christ Jesus as Lord, and ourselves as your bondservants for Jesus' sake." Burned-out people deny Christ as Lord—they are their own masters.

People who are burned out also *stop thinking biblically about their trials and difficulties.* In verses 7–9 Paul gives a marvelous illustration of what his life looked like through God's eyes, that is, an opportunity to be a witness to the greatest treasure there is: "But we have this treasure in earthen vessels, so that the surpassing greatness of the power will be of God and not from ourselves; we are afflicted in every way, but not crushed; perplexed, but not despairing; persecuted, but not forsaken; struck down, but not destroyed." Paul experienced persecution and affliction the likes of which most of us—by God's grace—will never begin to know. However, despite these problems, he was able to keep his life in perspective because he knew that God's good purposes were being accomplished by his trials. Because he knew that God would never forsake him, he did not despair. On the other hand, people who lose heart are people who feel the way that Paul described his life as being—afflicted in every way, perplexed, persecuted, struck down—but the difference is that they do despair and feel that God has forsaken them. They lose hope and allow themselves to be destroyed by their problems.

Not looking at problems biblically flows out of the loss of eternal perspective that we discussed in chapter 4. Paul said that he did not lose heart, for he remembered that "momentary, light affliction is producing for us an eternal weight of glory far beyond all comparison, while we look not at the things which are seen, but at the things which are not seen; for the things which are seen are temporal, but the things which are not seen are eternal" (2 Cor. 4:17–18). Burned-out people forget that the best is yet to come. They are shortsighted, looking only at the sometimes painful and difficult events of today, rather than being mindful of and focusing on future glory.

In verse 15 Paul said of his ministry, "For all things are for your sakes," because he knew that by serving others, he was really serving Christ. Jesus said, "To the extent that you did it to one of these brothers of Mine, even the least of them, you did it to Me" (Matt. 25:40). Paul called all believers to do the same, teaching and living the commandment, "You shall love your neighbor as yourself" (Gal. 5:14).

People who lose heart, however, fail to see service to others as being a great privilege. They no longer see their work as a means to glorify God as Paul did, "so that the grace which is spreading to more and more people may cause the giving of thanks to abound to the glory of God" (2 Cor. 4:15).

Burned-out people view their trials and difficulties selfishly, not biblically.

Finally, people who have lost heart *stop doing good.* In 2 Thessalonians 3:13 Paul gave this warning to those that might lose heart: "But as for you, brethren, do not grow weary of doing good." In a previous verse Paul said that he had heard that some of the Thessalonians were "leading an undisciplined life, doing no work at all, but acting like busybodies" (3:11). People who lose heart stop serving others and focus instead on themselves. They become complainers and busybodies, thinking about what others should be doing for them rather than what they should be doing for others and for God. Paul exhorted the Galatians in the same way: "Let us not lose heart in doing good, for in due time we will reap if we do not grow weary. So then, while we have opportunity, let us do good to all people, and especially to those who are of the household of the faith" (Gal. 6:9–10).

When people lose heart, they stop doing good to others. Paul repeated this phrase "doing good" several times in his epistles, but what does "doing good" involve? First Timothy 5:10 describes for us part of what it means to "do good." Paul taught Timothy that widows of a certain age were to be cared for by the church if they had a "reputation for good works." Paul went on to expound on what "good works" included: "If she has brought up her children, if she has shown hospitality to strangers, if she has washed the saints' feet, if she has assisted those in distress, and if she has devoted herself to every good work."

When people lose heart, they frequently cease doing these good works for others. Burned-out parents neglect their responsibility to care for their children. Burned-out people do not reach out to strangers. They do not perform menial tasks for the church and for other believers. They do not look for ways to help others who are in need, providing food and clothing and visiting the sick. They are not devoted to service or passionate about doing things for the Lord and for others.

Acts 9 describes a woman who did the kinds of good works that Paul mentioned in 1 Timothy 5. Luke wrote that Dorcas "was abounding with deeds of kindness and charity which she continually did" (9:36). In verse 39 Luke mentions at least some of her good works: "and all the widows stood beside [Peter], weeping and showing all the tunics and garments that Dorcas used to make while she was with them." Dorcas was skilled at sewing, and she apparently used that skill to serve the Lord by providing clothes for those in need. This woman had not lost heart in her ministry; she had not grown weary of doing good.

Hebrews 13:16 teaches us a little more about doing good: "And do not neglect doing good and sharing, for with such sacrifices God is pleased." Indeed, sharing with others is "doing good," and sharing that pleases God is sacrificial. In other words, God wants us to give to others not just out of our surplus, but to the point of sacrifice—meaning that it will cost us something.

If we study the previous verses in this passage, we learn that doing good also involves letting the "love of the brethren continue," showing hospitality to strangers, and remembering prisoners. It involves keeping our marriage vows and being sexually pure. It includes not being greedy and not making an idol of material things. It means encouraging and supporting the elders and other leaders of the church. And it involves following their example of godliness and not being carried away by false teachings (Heb. 13:1–9).

Still further, the writer of Hebrews said that it is a good work to be strengthened by grace and to continually offer up a sacrifice of praise to God. It is doing good to submit to leaders, especially the church leadership, and to pray for them because they keep watch over the souls of those to whom they minister. In fact, it is a good work to pray for all who minister the Word of God, that they may be kept pure and honorable in all things (Heb. 13:9–18).

People who have lost heart no longer do these good works, and so a lack of good works in someone's life is often a sign of a struggle with spiritual burnout. Lack of good works is really a symptom of a far greater problem. Though it is wrong for any believer to neglect good works, the heart problem of burnout that is behind this symptom is a most serious matter.

Burnout is a common problem, and it is a very serious problem. It has serious consequences for the lives of believers, and we must be on guard to not allow ourselves to give in to the temptation to lose heart. In the next two chapters we will study how to prevent spiritual burnout and we will also consider how to recover from spiritual burnout if we are already experiencing this problem in our lives (how to rekindle and maintain the flame of devotion and enthusiasm for Christ). God has a solution to the problem of burnout, and we can know and understand it if we are willing to let His Spirit work in our hearts and lives.

# APPLICATION

1. What symptom of burnout does the parable that Jesus taught in Luke 18 identify?

2. What are the four symptoms of spiritual burnout that Paul mentions in 2 Corinthians 4:1–2?

3. What do 2 Corinthians 4:7–9, 13, and 17–18 indicate often happens to people when they are experiencing spiritual burnout?

4. When a professing Christian stops or slows down in doing good works, what is one way of diagnosing and analyzing the reason for this stoppage or slowdown?

5. What symptoms of spiritual burnout are suggested by Galatians 6:9 and 2 Thessalonians 3:13?

6. What kinds of good works do people experiencing spiritual burnout stop doing?

7. Have you ever personally experienced any of the symptoms of spiritual burnout described in this chapter?
   a. Which of the symptoms mentioned in this chapter have you most often experienced?
   b. Were the symptoms mild, moderate, or severe?
   c. When you experienced these symptoms, did you understand that they might have been related to spiritual burnout?
   d. How can the information presented in this chapter about spiritual burnout be of practical help in your own life and in your ministry to others?

# 6

---

# THE GOOD NEWS
## ABOUT BURNOUT

In 2 Corinthians 4 Paul raises the issue of losing heart or what we're calling spiritual burnout. As we've looked at the context of this and other passages in Scripture, we have been confronted with the fact that spiritual burnout is a serious problem that brings with it many unfortunate consequences. Thankfully, however, Paul and the rest of the Bible writers don't merely describe the problem from a negative point of view. The Bible is replete with good news about preventing and overcoming spiritual burnout. The bad news is that we can experience spiritual burnout; the good news is that it can be both prevented and overcome.

Paul highlights the good news about this problem when he says, "we do not lose heart" (2 Cor. 4:1, 16). In other words, he avoided spiritual burnout. And, of course, the message Paul would want us to understand is that if he didn't lose heart, if he avoided spiritual burnout, we can too. And my friends, that's good news!

But there's more. The good news gets even better. The good news of the Bible not only includes the positive statement that spiritual burnout can be avoided; it includes information about how we can both avoid and overcome the downer experience of burnout. Thus far, we've seen that it's a very common and serious problem. Now we want to carefully examine what Paul and other Bible writers have to say about how to actually prevent and overcome spiritual burnout.

## FOUR IMPORTANT PRELIMINARY CONSIDERATIONS

However, before we actually explore this good news about how to avoid and overcome spiritual burnout, we need to be reminded of several things. First, note that the man who spoke about not losing heart was not a new Christian. When Paul wrote 2 Corinthians, he had been a Christian for at least twenty years. He had already completed two extensive missionary journeys, ministering to churches all over the region. His third and final missionary journey included many of the places that he had been to on his lengthy second trip. Second Corinthians was written in Macedonia on this third trip.

Often, new Christians are (rightly) excited about their new life in Christ. They find it easy to rejoice in all things. They are hungry for teaching, they eagerly accept new truths, and they are quick to tell others what they have learned. It is usually "older" Christians, people who have been believers for a period of time, who experience burnout as the trials and difficulties of life sap that initial excitement and zeal for the Lord. It is significant, then, that despite his many years in the faith—and innumerable trials and difficulties—Paul was still excited about the things of God and able to say, "We do not lose heart."

Second, the statement "we do not lose heart" was very significant in light of the fact that Paul had experienced a considerable amount of persecution during the time of his ministry. Four times in 2 Corinthians Paul writes about the difficulties he faced in his ministry. He first mentions them in chapter 1: "For we do not want you to be unaware, brethren, of our affliction which came to us in Asia, that we were burdened excessively, beyond our strength, so that we despaired even of life" (1:8). In chapter 4 he refers to the extensive afflictions, mistreatment, the stalking, the rejections, the continual danger and threats he experienced (4:7–17). In chapter 6, he again writes of experiencing afflictions, hardships, calamities, beatings, imprisonments, riots, labors, sleepless nights. And in the same chapter, he goes on to tell us that he has been dishonored, slandered, treated as an impostor, and punished. Finally, in chapter 11 Paul lists in some detail information about his various trials: imprisonments, beatings, stonings, lashings, shipwrecks, robberies, and on and on. While it is relatively easy for a believer who has never experienced difficulties to not lose heart because his faith has never been challenged, it is quite another matter for someone whose entire Christian life has been one of persecution and trial. Such was the life of the apostle Paul, and yet he was able to say—twenty years into his Christian life—"we do not lose heart."

Third, we must remember that Paul was not superhuman, nor was he devoid of feeling. On the contrary, this man experienced great physical weakness at times and was very sensitive emotionally. Now, I have known a few people who have an unusually steady emotional keel. They never seem to be down about anything. Nothing seems to cool their enthusiasm. In fact, I've known individuals who find it difficult to identify with people whose emotions tend to fluctuate. They can't understand why anyone would ever be tempted to experience burnout. Well, lest we think of Paul as one of these people, consider 2 Corinthians 1:23–2:4. In verse 23 Paul wrote, "But I call God as witness to my soul, that to spare you I did not come again to Corinth." He went on to explain the reason that he did not come: "For out of much affliction and anguish of heart I wrote to you with many tears; not so that you would be made sorrowful, but that you might know the love which I have especially for you" (2:4). Paul was so overcome with sorrow for these believers that he decided not to visit them so as not to burden them with his anguish.

Paul had good reason to be anguished by the Corinthians; they had been criticizing him, calling him untrustworthy, fickle, weak, ugly, and a poor speaker. Not only were they criticizing him, but they were sinning as well, and Paul knew that he had to deal with their sin. This too caused him sorrow, and so he told them, "But I determined this for my own sake, that I would not come to you in sorrow again" (2:1). Paul was a man of very deep feeling, and yet he could say: "we do not lose heart."

Fourth, as we consider this exhortation to not lose heart, we must keep in mind what Paul did and didn't say in these two verses (2 Cor. 4:1, 16). He did not merely say, "I do not lose heart," but "we do not lose heart." Paul wants us to know that he was not the only one who didn't lose heart. The "we" included at least Timothy, as 2 Corinthians 1:1 indicates. The fact that Timothy didn't lose heart is extremely significant in that 1 Corinthians 16:10–11 and several statements in the two letters (1 and 2 Tim.) Paul sent to him seem to indicate that he was a rather timid, sensitive person who by natural disposition could be susceptible to burnout. Beyond that, the "we" probably also included others such as Dr. Luke and the rest of the missionary team who usually traveled with Paul. Acts 20:4 records that Paul had several companions on his missionary journey: Sopater, Aristarchus, Secundus, Gaius, Timothy, Tychicus, Trophimus, and Luke (the author of Acts). Since all of these men were with Paul when he wrote 2 Corinthians and all of them to some extent experienced many of the things Paul experienced, the statement "*we* do not lose heart" is tremendously significant. Though each of these men was unique in his personality, weaknesses, and strengths, in spite of the hardships they had experienced, they had not suffered spiritual burnout.


## PAUL'S SECRET FOR OVERCOMING AND AVOIDING BURNOUT

These four points are important to keep in mind when considering Paul's statement about not losing heart. We are being instructed and encouraged by a man who was experienced in the faith, who knew difficulty, whose personality was deeply emotional, and who was accompanied by at least eight other believers who shared his zeal for the Lord. What was Paul's "secret"? How were he and his companions able to not lose heart under such circumstances and pressures?

The answer begins to unfold for us in Paul's words in 2 Corinthians 4:16: "Therefore we do not lose heart, but though our outer man is decaying, yet our inner man is being renewed day by day." Paul revealed that the secret to not losing heart was that he and his companions were experiencing constant spiritual renewal. This renewal occurs in the inner man in two ways.

### Requirements for Renewal

First, in order to not lose heart, we need the *renewal that comes at the time of salvation.* This initial renewing is described in Titus 3:5: "He saved us, not on the basis of deeds which we have done in righteousness, but according to His mercy, by the washing of regeneration and renewing by the Holy Spirit." When we are saved, God gives us a new heart, a new mind, and new goals for our life. Second Corinthians 5:17 says, "Therefore if anyone is in Christ, he is a new creature; the old things passed away; behold, new things have come."

Renewal of the inner man through salvation is the necessary foundation for all other spiritual work in us. Unless we come to faith in Christ, repenting of our sins and believing on Christ as Savior and Lord, we can never hope to prevent or overcome spiritual burnout. "[We] have put on the new self who is being renewed to a true knowledge according to the image of the One who created him" (Col. 3:10). The first step toward overcoming burnout is salvation. However, this initial renewal—though absolutely necessary—is not enough.

First Kings 19:8 records an unusual event in the life of the prophet Elijah: "So he arose and ate and drank, and went in the strength of that food forty days and forty nights to Horeb, the mountain of God." Now, God does not usually allow our bodies to be sustained for so long by one meal. Generally, we get no further than a few hours on one meal. Exodus 16 shows God's usual way of sustaining us. It describes how God provided the Israelites with manna every day and day to day, in order to teach them to depend on Him for their every need.

In the same way that we require a constant supply of physical food in order to sustain our outer man, we also need a constant supply of spiritual food to sustain our inner man. In other words, the renewal of salvation is just the beginning of a lifetime of living on the Word of God. "Man shall not live on bread alone, but on every word that proceeds out of the mouth of God" (Matt. 4:4). As believers, we need the sustenance of constant spiritual food as well as constant physical food. Failing to eat continuously of spiritual food leads to burnout.

In Colossians 2:6–7 Paul stated this principle of initial renewal through salvation that is followed by continuing renewal: "Therefore as you have received Christ Jesus the Lord, so walk in Him, having been firmly rooted and now being built up in Him and established in your faith" (Col. 2:6–7). We have been firmly rooted (past tense) at salvation, but then we must continue to walk (present tense) in Him and be built up (future tense) in Him.

It is interesting to note that many of the verbs used in the New Testament to describe the Christian life are in the present tense. For example, Romans 12:2 says, "And do not be conformed to this world, but be transformed by the renewing of your mind." Hebrews 12:1 says, "Let us run with endurance." And Luke 9:23 says, "If anyone wishes to come after Me, he must . . . take up his cross daily and follow Me." Not being conformed, being transformed, running, and taking up our cross are all things that we must do every day.

## RIGHT THINKING IS ESSENTIAL

Returning to the passage in 2 Corinthians 4, notice that Paul said, "Therefore we do not lose heart . . . our inner man is being renewed day by day" (4:16). "Day by day" indicates that renewal (keeping the flame burning brightly) is a continuing process, and therefore it requires continuing effort. Just as daily training is needed to keep the outer man in good physical shape, so also daily training is needed to keep the inner man in good spiritual shape. Athletes who take time off from training will begin to lose physical conditioning in a matter of only a few days. That is why true athletes commit themselves to exercise on a daily basis. True believers must have the same commitment to spiritual exercise.

Keeping the inner man in shape is also like maintaining a good marriage relationship. I have counseled couples who did not understand why, after ten years together, they could not stand each other anymore. They were at a loss to identify what happened, but the simple answer was that they stopped working on their relationship. A good marriage simply cannot be maintained unless it is worked on day by day, month by month, and year by year. The inner man requires constant work in the same way.

At this point we need to define what the "inner man" is. We have considered the fact that in order to not lose heart, we must be renewed day by day in our inner man, but what exactly is the "inner man"? The inner man comprises our thoughts, attitudes, emotions, feelings, desires, motives, goals, imagination, will, purposes, perspectives, and conscience. These are often summed up in Scripture by the word "mind," as in Romans 12:2: "And do not be conformed to this world, but be transformed by the renewing of your mind." Every day we must seek to renew our mind.

Every day we need to "let this mind be in [us], which was also in Christ Jesus" (Phil. 2:5, KJV). Daily we must "set [our] mind on the things above, not on the things that are on earth" (Col. 3:2). Day by day we must "[determine] to know nothing . . . except Jesus Christ, and Him crucified" (1 Cor. 2:2). We must continually follow the instruction of Colossians 3:16–17: "Let the word of Christ richly dwell within you, with all wisdom teaching and admonishing one another with psalms and hymns and spiritual songs, singing with thankfulness in your hearts to God. Whatever you do in word or deed, do all in the name of the Lord Jesus, giving thanks through Him to God the Father." Every day we must "lay aside every encumbrance and the sin which so easily entangles us, and . . . run with endurance the race that is set before us, fixing our eyes on Jesus . . . so that [we] will not grow weary and lose heart" (Heb. 12:1–3). If we are serious about avoiding the problem of spiritual burnout, we must be committed to daily renewal of our inner man.

Returning to 2 Corinthians 4, note that Paul made several points that speak specifically to this matter of daily renewal of the mind:

> But having the same spirit of faith, according to what is written, "I believed, therefore I spoke," we also believe, therefore we also speak, *knowing* that He who raised the Lord Jesus will raise us also with Jesus and will present us with you. (2 Cor. 4:13–14)

> For we *know* that if the earthly tent which is our house is torn down, we have a building from God, a house not made with hands, eternal in the heavens. (2 Cor. 5:1)

> Therefore, being always of good courage, and *knowing* that while we are at home in the body we are absent from the Lord—for we walk by faith, not by sight—we are of good courage. (2 Cor. 5:6–8)

Three times in these verses Paul uses the word "know." He says that because we know something, we do not lose heart. In other words, learning to think rightly is a means by which our minds are renewed.

Notice the present tense used in 2 Corinthians 10:5: "we are taking every thought captive to the obedience of Christ." Paul meant that every day, every hour, every minute there needs to be a conscious effort toward thinking biblically. This is very similar to what 1 Peter 1:13 says: "Therefore, prepare your minds for action, keep sober in spirit, fix your hope completely on the grace to be brought to you at the revelation of Jesus Christ."

Paul was teaching us to think—to not lose heart because we also can know something that he knew. What was it that Paul knew? First, Paul knew that *he had a very important ministry to perform for God.* In 2 Corinthians 4:1 he said, "Therefore, since we have this ministry, . . . we do not lose heart." Paul described something of this ministry in chapter 3. He called it a ministry "of the Spirit" and of "righteousness" (3:8–9). Paul knew that he had a job to do that was of eternal significance.

In 1 Timothy 1:12–14 Paul marveled at what a privilege it was to have been put into this ministry by God: "I thank Christ Jesus our Lord, who has strengthened me, because He considered me faithful, putting me into service, even though I was formerly a blasphemer and a persecutor and a violent aggressor. Yet I was shown mercy because I acted ignorantly in unbelief; and the grace of our Lord was more than abundant." Paul knew that God had ordained his ministry, and he also realized that he had done nothing to deserve such a high calling.

If we want to avoid losing heart, we must likewise know how important our ministries are and how dependent on God's grace we are for them. That alone is reason for excitement! It does not matter whether we see fantastic results or not. Paul acknowledged in his letters many times that the gospel that he preached was not always eagerly received: "And even if our gospel is veiled, it is veiled to those who are perishing, in whose case the god of this world has blinded the minds of the unbelieving so that they might not see the light of the gospel of the glory of Christ, who is the image of God" (2 Cor. 4:3–4).

Any ministry of God is a great privilege because it is for Him and because we are unworthy ministers. Paul knew that he was on a divine mission, and so are we. Jesus called us to be the salt of the earth and the light of the world; He called us to go into all the world and preach the gospel. Husbands have been called to help their wives to grow in Christ. Parents have been called to disciple their children. Pastors and teachers in the church have been called to equip the saints.

We, the saints, each have a high calling in Christ. Individually, God has given to each of us spiritual gifts, and He has commanded us to use these gifts for the edification of the church. "Since we have gifts that differ according to the grace given to us, each of us is to exercise them accordingly" (Rom. 12:6). We have been called to be living epistles in the world. We have been called to build up, encourage, and exhort fellow believers. Truly, as far as the church of God is concerned, there are no unimportant or insignificant people. Every child of God has an important ministry to fulfill in the body of faith.

Paul knew that he had an important ministry, and second, Paul knew that *he had "received mercy"* (2 Cor. 4:1). Paul recognized that he was like the publican in Luke 18:13, who stood in the temple, beat his chest, and said, "God, be merciful to me, the sinner!" Instead of giving Paul what he deserved—eternal damnation—God granted Paul mercy. God has granted us this same mercy, and we will not lose heart if we truly understand this mercy that we have received—undeserved, free, abundant, complete, bringing salvation and eternal glory.

How often do we lose heart because we think that we are not getting what we deserve? Whether it is fewer problems, less criticism, more success in our ministry, or more appreciation, we often allow our minds to dwell on things that we feel entitled to but that we are not receiving. When deprived of our perceived "rights," we become discouraged and lose heart because we are not thinking rightly.

Paul called us to *right thinking*. In contrast to our usual way of thinking, how often do our minds dwell on the fact that anything short of hell is far more than we deserve? The only thing that we deserve from God is eternal punishment for our sins. Any measure of grace and mercy from Him is far more than we deserve, and yet He has given to us *abundant* grace and mercy. Further, how often do we encourage our hearts by thinking about God rightly? Our God is a God of holiness, righteousness, mercy, and grace. If we want to avoid losing heart, we need to have a right view of ourselves and a right view of God.

Though God's mercy is just one aspect of His being, it was apparently the one that Paul thought about in particular so as not to lose heart. This was for good reason, since the Bible has much to say about the wonder of God's mercy. For example, in the twenty-six verses of Psalm 136, the psalmist makes this statement *twenty-six* times: "For his mercy endureth for ever" (KJV). This man was excited about the mercy of God: "O give thanks unto the LORD; for he is good: for his mercy endureth for ever" (Ps. 136:1, KJV). How often do we spend time thinking about God's mercy?

Lamentations 3:22–23 says, "Through the LORD's mercies we are not consumed, because His compassions fail not.

They are new every morning; great is Your faithfulness" (NKJV). God's great mercy can be a constant source of encouragement for us if we train ourselves to think about it regularly. In fact, in Romans 12:1 Paul mentions God's mercy in an appeal to us to live sacrificially: "Therefore I urge you, brethren, by the mercies of God, to present your bodies a living and holy sacrifice, acceptable to God, which is your spiritual service of worship."

If we want to avoid losing heart, then we must learn to think as Paul did. We have a divine ministry that we have received from God; that ought to encourage us greatly! God Almighty, Maker of heaven and earth, has chosen us to be His ministers. Not only that, but also this God is a God of great mercy. He has shown us mercy both in giving us salvation and in calling us to be His ministers.

Third, Paul did not lose heart because *he thought about God's present purposes for the problems of his outer man.* "But we have this treasure in earthen vessels, so that the surpassing greatness of the power will be of God and not from ourselves" (2 Cor. 4:7). "This treasure" is named in the previous verse. It is "the Light of the knowledge of the glory of God in the face of Christ." God could have used glorious vessels of silver or gold to house this great treasure, but instead He chose earthen vessels, or clay pots. We are those clay pots.

Why did God choose to put the great treasure of Jesus Christ into clay pots? Verse 7 says that He did it to show that all things are by His power, not by our power. A clay pot is a somewhat useful but not very durable container. It is easily chipped, cracked, even broken. So also, 2 Corinthians 4:16 says that "our outer man is decaying." As each of us already knows, our bodies experience all kinds of problems as we age and our physical strength diminishes.

I realize this more and more as I am now in the latter years of my life. For example, when my wife and I were in Maine with our oldest son and his family, one of my grand-daughters, who was ten, asked me to go down to the lake and watch the sunrise with her in the morning. At 5:15 the next morning, she was at my bedside to wake me. Though I had not slept well or long, I got up and went with her to the edge of the lake. I thought we were going to stand at the edge of the lake and wait for the sun to rise. But that's not what Ashley had in mind. When we got to the edge of the lake, she ran out on the narrow walkway about thirty or forty feet and then plopped down on a very narrow dock. Since I knew that I am not nearly as steady on my feet as I used to be, I came to the edge of the lake and just stood there surveying the scene and wondering if I should risk doing what Ashley had just done with great ease. As I stood there she turned to me and said, "Come on, Granddad. Come on out on the dock with me."

Well, what was I going to do? My sinful pride kept me from admitting to Ashley that I was a bit concerned that I might fall into the lake or that if I made it out on the dock without a mishap I might not be able to sit down on the dock or get up from the swaying dock after I got down.

I was too proud to admit my frailty to Ashley. Instead of telling her that Granddad was not as agile as he used to be and therefore would stand at the edge of the lake and watch the sunrise with her. I didn't want to disappoint her, so I carefully proceeded out on the walkway, which was rocking back and forth, praying all the while that God would help me not to fall in the water and make an absolute fool of myself in the presence of my granddaughter. I made it out to the dock and then just stood there for forty-five minutes while we watched the glorious spectacle together. I wanted so much to sit down as my feet were hurting me, but I didn't dare to do it because getting up without something to grab on to or without being able to turn over on my knees is a rather difficult task. I knew, as I stood there, that I could have easily sat down and gotten up just a few years before. I also knew then that I could no longer get down and get up as I once had because my outer man is decaying.

My body (and the body of every other believer) is and has always been just a clay pot. It's just that as we grow older, we become more and more aware of how frail these clay pots really are. But praise God, He has put the great treasure of Jesus Christ in our earthen vessels, in us fallible, frail, corruptible, and decaying human beings. He could have planned to use the holy, undefiled, incorruptible, glorious angels as the means to display the treasure. Instead, He chose to display and proclaim the glory of Christ through clay pots. And why did He choose to do it this way? He has done it this way for one purpose. God, says Paul, has put this treasure in us clay pots so "that the surpassing greatness of the power will be of God and not from ourselves" (4:7). God has deliberately chosen to use us, earthen vessels, so that whenever something is accomplished for the kingdom, people will see that we are not anything special and realize that it was done only by God's power. He has chosen to do it this way so that He will get the glory. He has chosen to do it this way so that His strength might be displayed through our weakness.

This is why Paul repeatedly rejoiced in his own weakness. Consider Paul's words in 2 Corinthians 12:9–10: "And He has said to me, 'My grace is sufficient for you, for power is perfected in weakness.' Most gladly, therefore, I will rather boast about my weaknesses, so that the power of Christ may dwell in me. Therefore I am well content with weaknesses, with insults, with distresses, with persecutions, with difficulties, for Christ's sake; for when I am weak, then I am strong." Because he knew that his weakness was a means of displaying Christ's strength, Paul did not become burned out during difficult times.

If we want to be like Paul and avoid losing heart in the midst of difficulties, if we want to rekindle and maintain the flame of devotion and enthusiasm for Christ, we must learn to think as Paul did. We need to renew our inner man daily by training our minds to think rightly about the things we've studied in this chapter. In the next chapter, we will consider one more thing that Paul thought about—his future prospects—and how focusing on this helped him to not lose heart. But for now, let's reflect and meditate on great truths we've learned from Paul in this chapter. Paul and his companions were kept from spiritual burnout by continuously reflecting and meditating on the importance of the ministry God had given to them, the greatness of God's mercy toward them, the great treasure that they had inside their decaying bodies, and the great privilege of displaying Christ's glory and power through their weakness and frailty. Reflecting on these truths was what helped Paul and his associates to be continuously renewed and refreshed in the inner man. In similar fashion, reflecting and meditating on these same great truths will also help us to avoid spiritual burnout.

## APPLICATION

1. What is the good news about spiritual burnout found in 2 Corinthians 4:1, 16?

2. As we consider the good news about spiritual burnout mentioned by Paul, what four things about Paul should we keep in mind?

3. What was Paul's "secret" for not being knocked down by spiritual burnout? How were he and his companions able to not lose heart under the circumstances and pressures they faced?

4. What is the necessary foundation, the first step, for avoiding spiritual burnout? What relevance do Titus 3:5–6 and Colossians 3:10 have in avoiding spiritual burnout?

5. What is the significance of the fact that many of the verbs used in the New Testament to describe the Christian life are in the present tense?

6. How is keeping the flame of faith and devotion to Christ burning brightly like what an athlete must do or like maintaining a good marriage relationship?

7. When Paul speaks of renewing the inner man, to what is he referring? What does he say needs to be renewed?

8. What does this fact about renewing the inner man indicate we must do if we are to avoid spiritual burnout? What is Paul calling us to?

9. What does Paul indicate that he and his associates continuously thought about that prevented them from experiencing spiritual burnout?

10. Why is our weakness a thing to rejoice about?

11. Write out 2 Corinthians 4:16 and work on memorizing it.

12. Do you regularly reflect on the truths presented in this chapter?

13. As you think about the fact that God has been merciful to you, that God has an important ministry for you, that God has given you a priceless treasure in Jesus Christ, and that your weakness is a cause for rejoicing in that it provides for you the wonderful opportunity for bringing glory to God, what effect does this have on you?

14. How can the information presented in this chapter about preventing spiritual burnout be of practical help in your own life and in your ministry to others?

# 7

## TALKING TO YOUR HEART

The secret to avoiding being knocked down by spiritual burnout, according to Paul in 2 Corinthians 4:16, is to have our inner man renewed daily. As we noted in chapter 6, this renewal begins at and with salvation (Titus 3:5–6), but it does not end there (2 Cor. 4:16). In fact, it is quite possible for people who have experienced initial renewal by salvation to experience burnout, or losing heart, if their inner man is not renewed daily. This does not mean repeated salvation, but rather a renewal of the mind through right thinking. In the previous chapter we noted several things that Paul thought about so that he would not lose heart. In this chapter I want to expand on one of the things we noted and then move on to consider another that Paul thought on that helped him and his associates not to lose heart.

Paul indicated that he did not lose heart because he knew some very important things: one, God had given him an important ministry; two, God had granted him great mercy; and three, God had a purpose for the problems of his outer man. In counseling, I am frequently asked the question "Why? Why did this happen to me?" People so often become depressed, confused, immobilized, bewildered, and even angry because they do not understand *why* something has happened to them. They imagine that if they could only understand the reason, it would be an easier burden to bear.

## THINK RIGHTLY ABOUT GOD'S PURPOSES

Though God does not always let us know His exact purposes in the events of our lives, we can be confident of this eternal truth: "And we know that God causes all things to work together for good to those who love God, to those who are called according to His purpose" (Rom. 8:28). "We who live are always being given over to death for Jesus' sake, so that the life of Jesus also may be manifested in our mortal flesh. . . . We have this treasure in jars of clay, to show that the surpassing power belongs to God and not to us. . . . For it is all for your sake, so that as grace extends to more and more people it may increase thanksgiving, to the glory of God" (2 Cor. 4:11, 7, 15, ESV). There were some things about what was happening to him that Paul didn't understand (2 Cor. 4:8); he admits that he was perplexed about some things. But there were other things about which he was not perplexed, about which he was absolutely sure. And one of those things was that somehow God was bringing glory to Himself through

Paul's difficulties and weaknesses, which meant that nothing he experienced—good or bad—was without reason.

Indeed, God often puts His children into difficult circumstances in order to bring glory to Himself by showing His strength through them. In 2 Corinthians 1:8 Paul writes that he and his companions experienced affliction "beyond our strength." This did not cause Paul to despair, but rather to trust even more in the power and strength of God. "We had the sentence of death within ourselves so that we would not trust in ourselves, but in God who raises the dead; who delivered us from so great a peril of death" (2 Cor. 1:9–10).

When we are at our weakest, the world is able to witness God's strength. In the midst of difficulties, we have the opportunity to be a powerful witness for Christ by the way that we handle those difficulties. Unbelievers frequently react to difficulties by becoming depressed, angry, anxious, and bitter; they feel overwhelmed. But when believers respond rightly in the midst of difficulties, it is a testimony to the power of God. When asked, "What makes you so different?" believers have the opportunity to share the reason for the hope that they have.

The first epistle of Peter is a wonderful book to study on the subject of suffering. Peter referred to suffering over fifteen times in this one book. He wrote about the past suffering of Christ and about the present suffering of believers. He made the point to his readers that if Christ, God's own Son, had to suffer, then we must "arm [ourselves] with the same way of thinking" (1 Peter 4:1, ESV). Back in chapter 3, Peter reminded his readers, "But even if you should suffer for the sake of righteousness, you are blessed. And do not fear their intimidation, and do not be troubled" (3:14). In other words, we should not lose heart because if our Savior had to suffer, then we should not expect to have a life without suffering. Paul knew, as Jesus had said, that as a servant of Jesus he was not above his Master; he knew that if Jesus, the Master, suffered, it was ludicrous to think that he would not have to suffer (John 15:18–19). He was absolutely convinced of this, and that helped him to rejoice even in his sufferings (Col. 1:24).

Paul knew that the sufferings of Jesus were not without purpose. He knew, as Peter said, that "Christ . . . suffered once for sins, the righteous for the unrighteous, that he might bring us to God" (1 Peter 3:18, ESV). He also knew, as stated in 2 Corinthians 4:11, that he was suffering for Jesus' sake: "For we who live are constantly being delivered over to death for Jesus' sake, so that the life of Jesus also may be manifested in our mortal flesh." Paul lived in constant danger of persecution and death in a way that most of us will never experience. In his day, there were no police forces to control angry mobs or arrest bandits and robbers. Paul had good reason to fear for his life, and yet he could still say that he did not lose heart.

In fact, Paul rejoiced that because of his suffering, others would be blessed. He was not a masochist who enjoyed pain and suffering, but he was a realist who understood that when handled properly his sufferings were a means of bringing blessing to people and glory to God. "For all things are for your sakes, so that the grace which is spreading to more and more people may cause the giving of thanks to abound to the glory of God" (2 Cor. 4:15). Paul knew that somehow God would use his difficulties for the benefit of other believers, and knowing that good purpose encouraged him. As believers, we have God's promise that "the LORD directs [our] steps" (Prov. 16:9) and "He knows the way [we] take; when He has tried [us, we] shall come forth as gold" (Job 23:10). Nothing happens in our lives by chance.

Not only does every step of our lives have a purpose in God's will, but as we noted earlier, God works all things together for "good to those who love God" (Rom. 8:28). Our trials may be for the benefit of others, but they are also for our own benefit. God uses our trials to refine us and make us more like Christ. All human events are governed by the sovereign will of God, which is good, acceptable, and perfect (Rom. 12:2). Knowing this, believing it, and reflecting on it will prevent spiritual burnout. It did for Paul and his associates, and it will for us also.

## KEEP THE BIG PICTURE IN MIND

Another matter on which Paul kept a godly perspective so as not to lose heart was *his future prospects.* Paul did not focus his mind on what was happening to him moment by moment, but instead he looked to the future and set his mind on the fact that the best was yet to come. In 2 Corinthians 4:17 Paul reflected that the present affliction was "producing for us an eternal weight of glory far beyond all comparison." He went on to say, "We look not at the things which are seen, but at the things which are not seen; for the things which are seen are temporal, but the things which are not seen are eternal" (4:18).

Returning to verse 17, it is interesting to note how Paul described his afflictions of the present. Clearly, he was training his mind to think properly when he wrote about "momentary, light affliction" because he knew that if he did not exercise control over his mind—if he allowed himself to think the way that the rest of the world thinks—he would lose heart.

Paul did not experience burnout because he thought of sufferings as being "momentary" and "light." From our earlier study, we know that Paul's afflictions hardly qualified as "light" if we judge them by any earthly standard. How then was he able to say they were "light"? He could say this because he measured his afflictions not against earthly standards, but against the future glory that is promised to all believers. "For I consider that the sufferings of this present time are not worthy to be compared with the glory that is to be revealed to us" (Rom. 8:18). He knew that there is no affliction on this earth that can compare with heavenly glory.

Paul said also that his present afflictions were "momentary" because he was again viewing them from God's perspective. In terms of his span of years on this earth, Paul's afflictions lasted a long time, but Paul did not measure them as the world would. Paul measured them against eternity and could rightly say that they, in fact, lasted but a moment.


## Stay Focused on the Right Thing

Not only did Paul view his afflictions as momentary and light, but Paul also considered the outcome of his afflictions: they were "producing for us an eternal weight of glory." He understood that his afflictions were of great benefit for the kingdom of God, and that encouraged him. As mentioned previously, Paul was not a masochist who got strange pleasure from pain for pain's sake. Paul simply rejoiced that his suffering was being used by God to further His kingdom. "For this reason I endure all things for the sake of those who are chosen, so that they also may obtain the salvation which is in Christ Jesus and with it eternal glory" (2 Tim. 2:10).

Paul's joy was not linked to earthly things, and therefore earthly forces could not take it away. The source of Paul's joy was his salvation in Jesus Christ, his promised inheritance in Christ, and the privilege of participating in the building of Christ's kingdom. "In this [we] greatly rejoice" (1 Peter 1:6), that we will "obtain an inheritance which is imperishable and undefiled and will not fade away, reserved in heaven for [us], who are protected by the power of God through faith for a salvation ready to be revealed in the last time" (1 Peter 1:4–5).

Paul agreed with Peter, who wrote that we have reason to rejoice "even though now for a little while, if necessary, you have been distressed by various trials" (1 Peter 1:6). Trials, though painful, are a necessary part of the Christian life because God has ordained them for a purpose. In fact, we can be assured that since God has ordained every trial that we experience, we can be assured that each one has a purpose. The purpose of these trials is revealed in 1 Peter 1:7: "That the proof of your faith, being more precious than gold which is perishable, even though tested by fire, may be found to result in praise and glory and honor at the revelation of Jesus Christ."

It is easy enough to claim faith when everything is going well, but true faith is constant regardless of circumstances. God uses trials in our lives to test the genuineness of our faith and to strengthen it. If our faith is lacking in any way, its weakness will be revealed in a time of trial. God allows our faith to be tested because the time to find out the measure of our faith is while we are still alive. After death, it is too late to discover that our faith has been false.

A popular bumper sticker reads: "Whoever dies with the most toys wins." The terrible truth, of course, is that whoever dies with only toys *loses everything.* Earthly treasure is dross that will be consumed in the fire of the judgment (1 Cor. 3:12–13). God demands genuine faith, not earthly toys. The bumper sticker should read: "Whoever dies with real faith wins." Paul knew that his trials had a purpose, and that helped him to not lose heart.

Not only did Paul know this, but he also focused his mind on it. And thus he declares, "We look not at the things which are seen, but at the things which are not seen" (2 Cor. 4:18). The Greek word *skopeō* that is translated "look" means to aim at, or focus one's attention on. None of the means for renewing the inner man that we have discussed in this and the previous chapter are automatic. There are many believers, including myself, who have at times become weary and lost heart because they were focusing their attention on the wrong things. We may know the truths of the Scripture, but it is quite another thing to focus our minds on them continuously.

Occasional focus—Sunday mornings, Wednesday evenings—is not enough because for the rest of the week, our thoughts will be elsewhere and thus we will lose heart. Paul knew the importance of right thinking; he knew the importance of continually thinking rightly (i.e., biblically); he knew the importance of thinking rightly about everything—past, present, and future; and he knew that right thinking doesn't just automatically happen, but is the result of disciplining the mind to think about the right things.

Philippians 3:12–14 is one of many passages in which Paul illustrates how he had disciplined his mind to think: "Not that I have already obtained it or have already become perfect, but I *press on* so that I may lay hold of that for which also I was laid hold of by Christ Jesus . . . ; but one thing I do: forgetting what lies behind and *reaching forward* to what lies ahead, I *press on toward* the goal for the prize of the upward call of God in Christ Jesus." Notice all the present-tense verbs in these verses: press on, reaching forward, and press on toward. Paul did these things every day, day after day. The result: he did not lose heart. He was steadfast in his faith because he had hope in what was to come. Hope is a critical, though often overlooked, part of the Christian life that we will consider in depth in chapter 12.

## THE ULTIMATE REASON FOR BURNOUT

In summary, losing heart is a result of unbiblical thinking. Because Paul disciplined his mind to dwell on the right things—his important ministry, God's great mercy toward him, the eternal purpose for the problems of his outer man, and his future prospects—he did not experience burnout. He talked to himself, as he instructed us to do, about the things that were true, honorable, right, pure, lovely, of good repute, excellent, and worthy of praise (Phil. 4:8).

In reality, we talk to ourselves all the time. Some of us do it quietly, so that others cannot hear, and some of us do it out loud. Sometimes it is a very conscious act, and sometimes we are hardly even aware that it is happening. Whether we realize it or not, however, it remains constant because that is the way our minds were designed. The Bible refers to this internal dialogue in many places. Psalm 14:1 says, "The fool has said in his heart, 'There is no God.'" Psalm 15:2 says, "He who walks with integrity, and works righteousness, and speaks truth in his heart."

The Bible addresses the subject of our internal dialogue for two reasons: one, it *reveals* the state of our *inner* man; and two, it *determines* the state of our *outer* man. Proverbs 4:23 says, "Watch over your heart with all diligence, for from it flow the springs of life." Psalm 19:14 says, "Let the words of my mouth and the meditation of my heart be acceptable in Your sight, O LORD, my rock and my Redeemer." A. W. Tozer wisely noted, "Anyone who wishes to check his true spiritual condition, may do so by noting what his voluntary thoughts have been over the last hours and day." Truly, an honest record of the natural wanderings of our mind on any given day is a good indication of the state of our inner man.

Jesus taught this very thing in Matthew 12:34–35: "For the mouth speaks out of that which fills the heart. The good man brings out of his good treasure what is good; and the evil man brings out of his evil treasure what is evil." He also said, "That which proceeds out of the man, that is what defiles the man. For from within, out of the heart of men, proceed the evil thoughts, fornications, thefts, murders, adulteries, deeds of coveting and wickedness, as well as deceit, sensuality, envy, slander, pride and foolishness. All these evil things proceed from within and defile a man" (Mark 7:20–23).

In other words, holiness and unholiness alike begin in the inner man. In his book *The Pursuit of Holiness* Jerry Bridges writes:

> It is time for us Christians to face up to our responsibility for holiness. Too often we say we are "defeated" by this or that sin. No, we are not defeated; we are simply disobedient! It might be well if we stopped using the terms "victory" and "defeat" to describe our progress in holiness. Rather we should use the terms "obedience" and "disobedience." When I say I am defeated by sin, I am unconsciously slipping out from under my responsibility. I am saying something outside of me has defeated me. But when I say I am disobedient, that places the responsibility for my sin squarely on me. We may, in fact, be defeated, but the reason we are defeated is because we have chosen to disobey. We have chosen to entertain lustful thoughts, or to harbor resentment, or to shade the truth a little.
>
> We need to brace ourselves up, and to realize that we are responsible for our thoughts, attitudes, and actions. We need to reckon on the fact that we died to sin's reign, that it no longer has any dominion over us, that God has united us with the risen Christ in all His power, and has given us the Holy Spirit to work in us. Only as we accept our responsibility and appropriate God's provisions will we make any progress in our pursuit of holiness.[1]

1. Jerry Bridges, *The Pursuit of Holiness* (Colorado Springs, Colo.: Navpress, 1996), 84–85.

What begins in our minds is worked out in our actions. As Jesus taught, if our hearts and minds are set on good things, then our actions will be good. If they are set on evil things, then our actions will be evil.

Any believer who is serious about avoiding burnout must take control of one's thoughts and train the mind to think biblically. Feelings, intuition, personal desires, the opinions of others—none of these are trustworthy unless they reflect the truth of the Word of God. In reality, feelings simply reflect the thoughts of the mind. The only way to know that the thoughts of our minds are right is to continually fill our minds with God's Word so that we can accurately evaluate our feelings, our circumstances, and the judgments of others.

Though the world teaches us to "listen to our hearts," as believers we need to "talk to our hearts." We need to do as Paul did: "whatever is true, whatever is honorable, whatever is right, whatever is pure, whatever is lovely, whatever is of good repute, if there is any excellence and if anything worthy of praise, dwell on these things" (Phil. 4:8). Our commitment to biblical "self-talk" is the key that will determine whether or not we experience burnout.

Any person who continuously thinks on the things that Paul's mind dwelt on will never experience spiritual burnout with its attendant consequences of instability, inconsistency, apathy, complacency, lethargy, and dryness. The flame of devotion and excitement can be maintained and, if it has been lost, rekindled by the strategies for renewal of the inner man used by the apostle Paul. We can be assured of this both by the promise of God and by the example of Paul's life. We do not have to lose heart! God has given us the solution to this heart problem as He has for every heart problem that we will ever face.

I would have despaired unless I had believed that I
would see the goodness of the LORD
In the land of the living.
Wait for the LORD;
Be strong and let your heart take courage;
Yes, wait for the LORD. (Ps. 27:13–14)


## APPLICATION

1. As we encounter hardship and difficulties in our lives, what are some of the things we can know for sure that will help us to prevent spiritual burnout?

2. Why did Peter say that if we suffer for the sake of righteousness, we are blessed?

3. Why did Paul say in Colossians 1:24 that he rejoiced in his sufferings?

4. What does it mean to suffer for Jesus' sake, and why should we consider this a blessing?

5. Why did Paul characterize his lengthy sufferings to be "light" and "momentary"?

6. What is meant by the statement "we talk to ourselves all the time"? How do we do this?

7. Why is what we think about so important? This chapter gives two reasons.

8. Summarize the meaning and gist of the Jerry Bridges quote in this chapter.

9. What is meant by listening to our hearts as opposed to talking to our hearts?

10. Write out 2 Corinthians 4:17–18 and work on memorizing these verses.

11. Do you regularly reflect on the truths presented in this chapter?

12. As you think about the fact that God has a good purpose for all the hardships we experience and focus on the wonderful future that is ahead for every Christian, what does this do for your inner man?

13. Make a list of as many of the wonderful blessings that we as Christians will experience in the future that can help make any afflictions we experience seem "light" and "momentary" by comparison.

14. How can the information presented in this chapter about preventing spiritual burnout be of practical help in your own life and in your ministry to others?

*Part 3*

# OTHER
# PROBLEMS

THAT KNOCK

YOU DOWN

# 8

## FEELING SORRY
## FOR YOURSELF

*Why me*?! How often have we asked this question, or at least been tempted to ask it, in the midst of difficulties? "Why is this happening to me? Why is God doing this to me? What did I do to deserve this?" Though we may not express them out loud, many of us have asked these questions in our hearts. The temptation to feel sorry for oneself is a common problem among Christians and non-Christians alike.

As a biblical counselor, I hear people ask these questions all the time. For example, a woman came to me and asked for help in coping with her children. Her children refused to listen to her; they mocked and cursed her. They threw stones at the neighbors' houses, and the neighbors complained to the police. She looked at me and cried, "Why me?" A young lady, looking around at her married or engaged friends, wondered, "Why me? Why don't I even have a boyfriend?"

Some students wonder why academics are such a struggle for them. Some spouses wonder why they cannot seem to make their marriage work. Some employees wonder why, after decades of service to one company, they are the first to be laid off. Some dieters wonder why they are always struggling with their weight. Some people wonder why a loved one—a parent, a spouse, a child—is taken from them at what seems a premature age. Indeed, the circumstances that lead us to ask "Why me?" are almost endless.

## BIBLICAL EXAMPLES OF WHY-ME PEOPLE

Similarly, the Bible indicates that many men of God struggled with the problem of feeling sorry for themselves. Moses asked some form of the "Why me?" question again and again in the book of Exodus. One of those times is recorded in chapter 5, when God sent Moses to Pharaoh to ask him to let the Israelites go into the desert to celebrate a feast to Him. Pharaoh responded by increasing the Israelites' workload, since they apparently had too much time on their hands if they were asking to have a feast in the wilderness. This, of course, greatly upset the Israelites, who became quite angry with Moses for increasing their already difficult labor. "They said to [Moses and Aaron], 'May the LORD look upon you and judge you, for you have made us odious in Pharaoh's sight and in the sight of his servants, to put a sword in their hand to kill us' " (5:21). Moses' immediate reaction to this was self-pity. "Then Moses returned to the LORD and said, 'O Lord, why have You brought harm to this people? Why did You ever send me?' " (5:22).

Elijah asked nearly the same thing of God in 1 Kings 19. Elijah had been sent by God to live by the brook Cherith where he was fed by ravens (1 Kings 17:1–5). There was a drought in the land, and eventually the little stream that God had provided for Elijah dried up. God then sent him to live with a poor widow in Sidon. After living with her for a while, he was sent by God to rebuke Ahab, Jezebel, and the priests of Baal for their idolatry.

In 1 Kings 18 Elijah called down fire from heaven to consume his sacrifice and to demonstrate God's power over the impotence of Baal. Despite the impressive show, Ahab and Jezebel were unmoved and threatened Elijah with his life. Elijah ran into the wilderness, collapsed under a juniper tree, and cried to God, "It is enough; now, O LORD, take my life, for I am not better than my fathers" (1 Kings 19:4). In other words, "Why me?"

Frequently, the writers of the psalms asked the question "Why me?" Psalm 73 is one of those psalms, and I believe that this particular psalm is especially instructive because not only does it show a man who is struggling with self-pity, but it also reveals the solution that this man found for dealing with his self-pity. God has a solution for the problem of self-pity, just as He does for all our other problems, and this psalm reveals what that solution is.

Psalm 73 begins with these words: "Surely God is good to Israel, to those who are pure in heart! But as for me, my feet came close to stumbling, my steps had almost slipped." Whether this man was experiencing physical and spiritual weakness or just speaking metaphorically about his spiritual weakness, we are not told, but he was in trouble either way. Later verses reveal the self-pity in his heart. "Surely in vain I have kept my heart pure and washed my hands in innocence; for I have been stricken all day long and chastened every morning" (vv. 13–14).

This man was clearly feeling sorry for himself, and these words—along with those that describe his eventual restoration—are included in the Word of God for our instruction. In 1 Corinthians 10:11 Paul comments, "Now these things happened to them as an example, and they were written for our instruction." I believe that this psalm, Psalm 73, was included in the Scripture to teach us how to deal rightly with the problem of self-pity. "All Scripture is . . . profitable for teaching, for reproof, for correction, and for training in righteousness" (2 Tim. 3:16).

## The Unanswerable and Useless Question

It is important to note, however, before we begin to look at God's solution that the problem of self-pity cannot be dealt with directly. In other words, God does not want us to deal with this problem by attempting to actually *answer* the question "Why me?" As we study this psalm, we will not find a list of reasons for our problems or an explanation of why we deserve whatever we are experiencing.

Most secular counselors—and some Christian counselors as well—deal with self-pity in precisely that way. They attempt to help people understand the "why" in the hope that this knowledge will then allow them to overcome their problems. For example, they believe that if people know *why* they are always angry, they can then overcome their anger. Or, if individuals know *why* they are depressed, they can then overcome their depression. Unfortunately, knowing the reasons for our problems does not usually solve them.

I once counseled a woman who had previously wasted thousands of dollars and several years on secular psychology. Instead of getting better, she told me, "I am a more intelligent but still miserable person." What she meant was that although she "knew" in some manner more about her problem, she was no closer to overcoming it than she ever was. On the basis of our sessions together, I would say that she was right. She was a truly miserable woman, and no one's attempt to explain to her why she was miserable had lessened her misery one bit.

Not long ago, I counseled a man who began by saying to me, "I have come because I want you to tell me why a certain thing has happened to me." After he explained what had happened to him, I replied, "Supposing I could tell you why it happened; how would that help you to *deal with* what happened to you?" I continued by explaining to him that knowing why something has happened in our lives does not change its reality, nor does it help us to deal with it. Instead of asking "Why?" what we should be asking is, "Now that this has happened, how should I handle it? What should my response to this situation be?" Together we looked at Deuteronomy 29:29, which says, "The secret things belong to the LORD our God, but the things revealed belong to us and to our sons forever, that we may observe all the words of this law." I challenged my counselee that what he ought to be concerned with was what God says about his situation and how God says he should respond to it.

Only God knows the answers to all the whys of our lives. Proverbs 20:24 says, "Man's steps are ordained by the LORD, how then can man understand his way?" We are free to speculate on why things happen to us, but none of us will ever know for sure unless God reveals His purposes to us in heaven someday in the future. Rather than attempting to answer the unanswerable question "Why me?" we should be focusing instead on what God says in His Word about responding to and handling our problems.

## THE REAL CAUSES OF SELF-PITY

That is exactly what happens with the self-pitying author of Psalm 73. As we study this psalm, we will consider its teaching in two parts. First, we will look at the description of the causes of self-pity in verses 2–14. Then, we will look at the cure for self-pity that is demonstrated in verses 15–28. In order to understand this problem of self-pity better, we will look at the causes first and then the cure.

The first contributing problem to the psalmist's self-pity is mentioned in verse 3: "For I was envious of the arrogant as I saw the prosperity of the wicked." This man was struggling with self-pity *because of his sinful envy.* James 3:16 warns, "For where jealousy and selfish ambition exist, there is disorder and every evil thing." Proverbs 14:30 teaches, "A sound heart is life to the body, but envy is rottenness to the bones" (NKJV). According to the Word of God, envy is evil and causes destruction.

What is envy? Envy begins with a strong desire for what someone else has. For example, in Genesis 30:1 it is recorded that Rachel was envious of her sister Leah because she could not have children and Leah could. "[Rachel] became jealous of her sister; and she said to Jacob, 'Give me children, or else I die.' " Her desire for a child had overwhelmed her heart to the point that she felt that she would die if she did not have one. Envy is more than just a desire for what someone else has, however. Envious people think that they *deserve* to have what someone else has, just as much as or even more than the other person deserves to have it.

That was how Rachel felt about having a child, and that was also how the psalmist felt in Psalm 73. Consider his words in verse 3: "I was envious of the arrogant as I saw the prosperity of the wicked." He goes on to describe how these people are proud, violent, mockers, irreligious, blasphemers, and wicked (vv. 5–9). Yet, he says, they prosper. "Behold, these are the wicked; and always at ease, they have increased in wealth" (v. 12). Then, in verse 13, he complains that all his righteousness has gotten him nothing.

In addition to envy, I believe that the psalmist was struggling with self-pity *because of his sinful exaggeration.* He exaggerated the extent of his own problems, and he really exaggerated the prosperity of the wicked. In fact, three times in this psalm he exaggerated the prosperity of the wicked.

First, he claims, "For there are no pains in their death" (v. 4). As a minister, I have been at the bedside of unsaved people as they were dying, and I can attest to the pain of death that I have witnessed. He exaggerates again in the second part of verse 4: "And their body is fat." Later, he adds, "Their eye bulges from fatness" (v. 7). What he means is that they have more food than they can eat, but that is not true of all unsaved people either. There are many ungodly people in the world who are starving, and there were starving, ungodly people in the psalmist's day as well. He was exaggerating their prosperity—their comfort in death and their excess of provisions—because he pitied himself.

He also minimized the extent to which they experienced difficulties in their lives: "They are not in trouble as other men, nor are they plagued like mankind" (v. 5). In other words, he claimed that wicked people did not have problems. As a biblical counselor who has worked with many people—believers and nonbelievers—I can say with confidence that there is *no one* who does not have problems. In fact, many people have terrible problems.

Not only did the psalmist exaggerate the prosperity and ease of the wicked, but he exaggerated his own problems as well. "Surely in vain I have kept my heart pure and washed my hands in innocence" (v. 13). The words "in vain" mean "for nothing." In other words, this man claimed that living for God had profited him *nothing*. That, of course, was a lie. He had received blessings as a child of God, and he remembered and declared those blessings later in the psalm.

At this point, however, he was so overwhelmed by his self-pity that all his thoughts about his troubles had crowded out any thoughts about his blessings. In fact, in verse 14 he complains, "For I have been stricken all day long and chastened every morning." Again, I believe that he was exaggerating his troubles because his self-pity had distorted his thinking. Exaggeration and distorted thinking are problems that often accompany self-pity because a person who is focused on the question "Why *me?*" is clearly focused on self.

The third reason that this man was struggling with self-pity was *his confusion about the nature and source of true blessing.* He said, "I saw the prosperity of the wicked" (v. 3), but what he saw was not true prosperity. God promises in His Word that His children will be prosperous and rich. For example, in Psalm 1:3 God pledges that the godly person "will be like a tree firmly planted by streams of water, which yields its fruit in its season and its leaf does not wither; and in whatever he does, he prospers." Second Corinthians 8:9 similarly promises, "For you know the grace of our Lord Jesus Christ, that though He was rich, yet for your sake He became poor, so that you through His poverty might become rich." The Bible promises both prosperity and riches to those who know God, and we know that God keeps His promises.

So why aren't we all driving Bentleys and living in mansions? Why aren't we all dripping with gold and jewels? I have counseled many people who have seriously wondered about that. They wonder because they have misunderstood the nature of the prosperity and riches that God promises to those who love Him. The writer of Psalm 73 likewise misunderstood the nature of God's riches when he was jealous of the "prosperity" of the wicked. He demonstrated his misunderstanding by focusing on the "fatness" of the wicked.

The Bible makes it very clear that God's riches are not material things. In Luke 12:15 Jesus taught, "for not even when one has an abundance does his life consist of his possessions." In Matthew 16:26 He asked, "For what will it profit a man if he gains the whole world and forfeits his soul?" Our relationship with Christ is far more valuable than all the money in the world because only that relationship can save us from eternal damnation. The person whose eternity is secure is rich indeed!

Psalm 19 teaches that the law, testimony, precepts, commandments, fear, and judgments of the Lord are "more desirable than gold, yes, than much fine gold; sweeter also than honey and the drippings of the honeycomb" (vv. 7–10). Proverbs 3:13–18 expresses the same thought:

> How blessed is the man who finds wisdom
> And the man who gains understanding.
> For her profit is better than the profit of silver
> And her gain better than fine gold.
> She is more precious than jewels;
> And nothing you desire compares with her.
> Long life is in her right hand;
> In her left hand are riches and honor.
> Her ways are pleasant ways
> And all her paths are peace.
> She is a tree of life to those who take hold of her,
> And happy are all who hold her fast.

God's prosperity and riches are His wisdom, His salvation, and His joy in our hearts. These things are far more valuable than any earthly riches—than *all* earthly riches—and He surely keeps His promise to give us these things. The psalmist was feeling sorry for himself because he misunderstood the nature of God's prosperity.

Finally, this man was struggling with self-pity *because of his sinful fretting*. "Fretting" is becoming so preoccupied with a problem that our thoughts about it consume nearly all our thinking. In Psalm 37 God commands "Fret not" three times in the first eight verses. In His Word, God deals with the problem of fretting because so many of us are guilty of this sin.

A woman once sat in my office and wept over something rather trivial that she had done to her son thirty years earlier. When her son became an Eagle Scout, she had planned a party to celebrate, but had not thought to ask her son what kind of party he wanted. She fretted over that mistake and some others like it for decades afterward, constantly churning in her mind how she had not done everything for her children that she wanted to do for them.

People fret over both big things and little things, but regardless of the size of the problem, fretting inhibits people from serving the Lord effectively because it completely distracts their minds from the things of the Lord. The writer of Psalm 73 had his mind focused on the prosperity of the wicked and his own lack of prosperity. These thoughts consumed him for a while, and he was therefore unable to think of anything else but "Why me?"

### THE REAL CURE FOR SELF-PITY

Many sins contribute to feeling sorry for oneself—envy, exaggeration, misunderstanding true prosperity, and fretting—but this psalm provides us with much more than just the causes of this problem. By God's grace, the writer of this psalm found and recorded God's solution to his problem. The first part of the cure for self-pity is in verse 15: "If I had said,

'I will speak thus,' behold, I would have betrayed the generation of Your children." The first means of overcoming self-pity is *exercising self-control over our words*. In verse 15 the psalmist abruptly takes control of himself. After writing about his misery for a while, he seems to have suddenly changed course and decided that what he had been doing was wrong. Realizing the importance of guarding his tongue, he takes control of his words so that he will not sin further or cause others to sin. Proverbs 10:19 teaches, "When there are many words, transgression is unavoidable, but he who restrains his lips is wise," and Proverbs 13:3 counsels, "The one who guards his mouth preserves his life; the one who opens wide his lips comes to ruin."

Many people, even believers, seem to be ignorant of the wisdom of this teaching and chatter on and on about their problems to anyone unfortunate enough to ask or listen. Instead of bringing about change, this constant rehashing of problems does nothing but encourage despair and self-pity. Overcoming self-pity requires a bridle on the tongue. We cannot expect to experience hope, encouragement, and peace if our mouth is constantly spewing forth despair, discouragement, and woe.

Overcoming self-pity involves *exercising control over our thoughts as well*. In verse 15, the psalmist appears to have realized this and changed his thinking. So he writes, "Behold, I would have betrayed the generation of Your children." In other words, he took control of his mind and began to think about what was beneficial for others rather than about his own miseries. He became convicted about the sin of "spouting off" and about the negative influence his words might have on others.

Philippians 2:4 says, "Do not merely look out for your own personal interests, but also for the interests of others." Instead of focusing on ourselves, we need to think about the potential damage that our sin could do in the lives of others. Our complaining can be a stumbling block to those around us, possibly tempting them to sin as well. This is what the psalmist realized in verse 15, and when he began to turn his thoughts away from himself and toward others and their needs, self-pity started to loosen its grip on his heart and mind.

This is the first part of overcoming self-pity: exercising control over our thoughts and words so that they become pleasing to God and helpful to others. Paul reminded us of this important truth in Romans 14:7–8: "For not one of us lives for himself, and not one dies for himself; for if we live, we live for the Lord; therefore whether we live or die, we are the Lord's."

The second part of overcoming self-pity is going to "the sanctuary." "When I pondered to understand this, it was troublesome in my sight" (v. 16). In other words, the psalmist came to the place in his thinking where he realized his own inadequacy in answering his questions. At that point he decided to enter the sanctuary of God—the place of God's Word, of prayer, of meditation, and of God's people—in order to find understanding. The psalmist was troubled by the prosperity of the wicked "until I came into the sanctuary of God; then I perceived their end" (v. 17). He then goes on to describe the things that he began to understand after entering the sanctuary.

First, he understood the real condition of the ungodly: "Surely You set them in slippery places; You cast them down to destruction" (v. 18). He recognized that wicked people were not in enviable places but rather in unstable and insecure places. "How they are destroyed in a moment! They are utterly swept away by sudden terrors!" (v. 19). He realized that they were not in peace or free of pain, but rather in great emotional distress. "Like a dream when one awakes, O Lord, when aroused, You will despise their form" (v. 20). He saw that the wicked live in a fantasy world of their own making because there is no reality apart from Christ.

He understood also that the future of the ungodly was destruction. "You cast them down to destruction. How they are destroyed in a moment!" (vv. 18–19). As the Scripture teaches in John 3:36, "He who believes in the Son has eternal life; but he who does not obey the Son will not see life, but the wrath of God abides on him." The writer of Hebrews warned, "And inasmuch as it is appointed for men to die once and after this comes judgment" (9:27). Truly, the wicked will not escape eternal judgment at the hand of God no matter how comfortable or miserable their life on earth is.

Not only did the psalmist begin to understand the real condition of the ungodly, but he also began to understand that he was ultimately responsible for his own struggle with self-pity. "When my heart was embittered and I was pierced within, then I was senseless and ignorant; I was like a beast before You" (vv. 21–22). According to Hebrew-language scholars, the verbs in verse 21 are reflexive; in other words, the verse might better be translated: "When I embittered my heart and I pierced myself within. . . ."

As his understanding increased, the psalmist recognized that he was causing his own problems with his sinful thoughts. The real problem was not that the wicked seemed to prosper or that his life had problems. *The real problem was that he was not thinking rightly about his situation.* He was embittering his own heart and causing his own pain by his "senseless and ignorant" thinking (v. 22). Instead of looking at life from God's perspective, he was looking at life as an animal would, from a purely physical and materialistic perspective.

Accepting responsibility for our problems is key to overcoming self-pity. Self-pity is not caused by our problems; it is caused by our *reactions* to our problems. Until the psalmist stepped outside of his woes and into the sanctuary of God, he was unable to react to his problems correctly. We also must find understanding by being willing to go to the sanctuary of God's Word, prayer, meditation, and Christian fellowship so that we will be able to look at life from God's perspective.

The third part of overcoming self-pity is understanding and meditating on the wonderful privileges that are ours as children of God, regardless of our external circumstances. In verses 23–28 the psalmist listed just a few of the countless blessings that we enjoy as God's children. He mentioned the blessing of always being with God and having His support and comfort: "Nevertheless I am continually with You; You have taken hold of my right hand" (v. 23). He wrote about the blessing of having God's guidance: "With Your counsel You will guide me" (v. 24a). He realized the blessing of eternal security: "and afterward receive me to glory" (v. 24b). He acknowledged the blessing of divine strength: "My flesh and my heart may fail, but God is the strength of my heart and my portion forever" (v. 26). He mentioned the blessing of God's sufficiency: "Whom have I in heaven but You? And besides You, I desire nothing on earth" (v. 25). And he realized the blessing of divine protection: "But as for me, the nearness of God is my good; I have made the Lord GOD my refuge" (v. 28).

Finally, the writer remembered and declared his true purpose in life, "that I may tell of all Your works" (v. 28). He said that his purpose for living was to glorify God. Many people in this world have no purpose for their lives; they have no idea why they were created and why they exist. In my counseling work, I often hear miserable people ask the question, "Why am I here?" They realize, correctly, that if life has no purpose, then we are to be greatly pitied because everything that we do is in vain.

No child of God need live with that kind of misery, however. We have a very clear purpose in life as Christians: "For we do not preach ourselves, but Christ Jesus the Lord, and ourselves your bondservants for Jesus' sake. For it is the God who commanded light to shine out of darkness, who has shone in our hearts to give the light of the knowledge of the glory of God in the face of Jesus Christ" (2 Cor. 4:5–6, NKJV). Our purpose in life is to glorify God in everything that we do and preach the gospel to every person on earth. In 1 Corinthians 10:31 Paul taught, "Whether, then, you eat or drink or whatever you do, do all to the glory of God." And Jesus said, "Go into all the world and preach the gospel to every creature" (Mark 16:15, NKJV).

Overcoming self-pity is really a matter of changing our hearts by changing our minds. It requires a change in thinking: exercising control over our words and our thoughts, going to the sanctuary of God's Word for wisdom and understanding, and meditating on our privileges as God's children. Believers whose lives are characterized by these things will not succumb to the temptation to ask "Why me?" no matter what the circumstances of their lives might be, for their hearts and minds will be filled up to overflowing with the knowledge of God.

## APPLICATION

1. Take a few minutes to think back through the last few months. Write down the times that you remember being tempted to feel sorry for yourself and ask "Why me?"

2. Evaluate what the operative causes of your self-pity were.
   a. Were you struggling with envy? Whom were you envying?
   b. Were you struggling with exaggeration of your or someone else's circumstances?
   c. Were you struggling with misinterpreting the nature of true blessing?
   d. Were you struggling with fretting? What were you fretting about?
   e. What steps do you need to take, or have you taken, in order to deal with these sins?

3. Evaluate your self-control.
   a. Do you bridle your tongue like the psalmist in Psalm 39, or are you like the fool in Proverbs 29:11, who says exactly what he is thinking?
   b. Do you exercise self-control over your thoughts as Paul instructed in Philippians 4:8?

4. Evaluate your sense of responsibility. Do you blame your negative responses to problems on those who cause them (spouse, children, parents, environment, job,

neighbors, etc.), or do you take full responsibility for your responses to problems, regardless of their cause?

5. Use a concordance (the one in the back of your Bible or a separate, more complete concordance) to help you find everything you can about what the Bible has to say about the condition of the "ungodly" or the "wicked." Write down and firmly fix in your mind what God's perspective is on their condition.

6. Use the concordance to help you find everything that the Bible has to say about the privileges of God's children. Write down and meditate on what God's perspective is on your life.

7. Read through Psalm 73.
   a. Write a paragraph on each of the blessings mentioned in this chapter that the psalmist reminds himself about. Describe what each one means and what its implications are for your life.
   b. Make a list of the ways that you can fulfill God's purpose for your life by reaching others for Christ.

8. How can you use the truths presented in this chapter to help you or someone else when feeling sorry for self becomes a serious temptation?

# 9

---

# DISCONTENTMENT

Famine, persecution, poverty, physical abuse, serious illness, imprisonment—people all over the world are experiencing, or have experienced, extremely difficult circumstances such as these. I wonder how many of those people, or even people whose problems are trivial in comparison (like many of us), could make a statement like Paul's in Philippians 4:10–13:

> But I rejoiced in the Lord greatly, that now at last you have revived your concern for me; indeed, you were concerned before, but you lacked opportunity. Not that I speak from want, *for I have learned to be content in whatever circumstances I am.* I know how to get along with humble means, and I also know how to live in prosperity; in any and every circumstance I have

learned the secret of being filled and going hungry, both of having abundance and suffering need. I can do all things through Him who strengthens me.

Paul said that he had learned to be content in *any* circumstance. This is a remarkable statement, yet he was completely serious and honest when he made it. We know this because Paul was writing by the inspiration of the Holy Spirit of God, whose Word is truth.

If most of us were to honestly evaluate our level of contentment in life, we would more likely say something like this: "I'm sometimes content, but it depends on my mood at the time," or "I'm seldom content, no matter what my circumstances are." And there are some people who are *never* content with anything. If it's raining, they wish it were sunny. If it's sunny, they want it to be cooler. Their small car doesn't have enough power, but their big car uses too much gas. They never have enough money, or the right kind of job, or a big enough house, or enough time off. I once saw a cartoon in which a husband was yelling at his wife, "You don't want to keep up with the Joneses, you want to *be* the Joneses!" Some people are actually never content, no matter what their circumstances are.

Most of us, however, could honestly say, "I am content under *certain* circumstances." We are content when we are healthy, or when we have enough money to buy what we want, or when our job is going well, or when our family is happy. We are content when we are well liked and appreciated and when people do what we want. We are content when no one criticizes or disagrees with us. If any of these things change, however, our contentment falters.

When the apostle Paul wrote that he had learned to be content in *any* circumstance, he was not writing from a presidential palace, with servants waiting on him hand and foot. The apostle Paul most likely wrote this letter to the Philippians from Rome, at the end of his third missionary journey, while under house arrest and awaiting trial. By this time in his life, he had traveled widely and had known just about every condition of life possible.

As a young man, Paul had been instructed by one of the leading rabbis of that time, Gamaliel. Paul was known to be a well-educated, zealous, and intelligent Hebrew with the added distinction of Roman citizenship by birth. Before his conversion he was considered to be a rising star among the religious leaders of the day. Even after his conversion there were a few occasions during his ministry when Paul was highly praised or revered.

Acts 14 records one of these occasions. During his first missionary journey, Paul healed a lame man in Lystra. When the people saw this man, who had been lame from birth, jump up and walk around, they were amazed by what Paul had done (Acts 14:8–10). "They raised their voice, saying . . . , 'The gods have become like men and have come down to us.' And they began calling Barnabas, Zeus, and Paul, Hermes, because he was the chief speaker. The priest of Zeus . . . wanted to offer sacrifice with the crowds" (14:11–13).

Paul was hailed as a god again in Acts 28 after being bitten by a snake. When the people around him saw that he suffered no ill effects from the bite, "they changed their minds and began to say that he was a god" (28:6). Later, after Paul had healed several people in that area who were sick, Luke wrote that "they also honored us with many marks of respect; and when we were setting sail, they supplied us with all we needed" (28:10).

Such praise and honor were hardly the norm for Paul during his ministry, however, as the rest of Acts and Paul's epistles reveal. He experienced ridicule, imprisonment, beating, stoning, shipwreck, hunger, sleeplessness, exposure to extreme weather, robbery, and countless other perils (2 Cor. 11:23–27). Yet through all these experiences—good and bad, easy and difficult—Paul could say near the end of his life: "I have learned to be content."

## TRUE CONTENTMENT MUST BE LEARNED

The Greek word translated "content" in Philippians 4:11 is *autarkēs*, but there is another Greek word that is also translated "content." It is the related word *arkeō*. Paul used this second word in 1 Timothy 6:8: "If we have food and covering, with these we shall be *content*." The word *arkeō* literally means "to be self-sufficient." In other words, Paul had learned to be independent of his circumstances. He had learned to not let people or events control him, determine his misery or his joy, or inhibit his ministry.

In that sense, Paul had discovered the secret of true freedom. He was satisfied at all times, in all places, and in all ways in Christ. We might wonder why Paul felt it necessary to brag about his "superhuman" ability to cope with difficulties, but if we did, we would be missing the point of his words in Philippians 4. Since everything in the Word of God is included for our benefit (Rom. 15:4), the Holy Spirit wants us to know that *we have the power and the ability* to live as Paul did. The point is that *we too* can learn to be content in whatever circumstances we find ourselves.

When I ask people how they are doing, I am often answered with something like this: "Pretty well, under the circumstances." I wonder then—as I imagine Paul would also—what they are doing *under* their circumstances. We should not be *under* our circumstances; as believers, we should be *above* our circumstances. In other words, we should be living independently of what is happening to us—rejoicing in the Lord and content with whatever He sees fit to bring into our lives.

Before we continue, it is important to note that this teaching in Philippians 4 does not mean that we should never seek to change or improve our circumstances. This teaching is not a prohibition against seeing the doctor when we are sick, studying harder for a better grade, practicing harder to improve a skill, or working harder to get a raise or promotion. What it does mean is that after we have done whatever is required or appropriate to improve our circumstances or to improve the world around us, we must leave the final outcome in God's hands. It means that after we have done everything possible to get well, we must be content with our health whether we improve or not. It means that after we have studied our best, practiced diligently, and worked our hardest, we must be content with whatever God brings about. It also means that while we are continually thankful to God for His provision of health, education, talents, jobs, and countless other blessings, we are never so dependent on these things that if they were taken away, we would be discontent.

When Paul said that he was "content in whatever circumstances," he meant that whatever he was given by God was sufficient for him. If everything had changed the very next day, he would still have been content because his security was in Christ. As Peter said, "His divine power has granted to us everything pertaining to life and godliness, through the true knowledge of Him who called us by His own glory and excellence" (2 Peter 1:3). Paul was content because he had everything he needed in Christ.

## DISCOVERING PAUL'S "SECRET"

Many of us would like to be more content. We realize that as believers, we should be less emotionally tied to the things of this world. We would like to be above our circumstances and to not have emotional ups and downs according to the ups and downs of our lives. But some of us may be thinking, "I've really tried to be content, but I just *can't*." Did Paul have special powers? What was his secret?

Paul revealed an important aspect of true contentment when he said, "For I have *learned* to be content. . . . I have *learned the secret* of being filled and going hungry"— contentment must be learned. The fact that we are not content now does not mean that we are not capable of it; it just means that we have not yet learned how.

As believers, we are not automatically endowed with perfect contentment in our lives. Just like Paul, we must *learn to be content.* But how do we learn? How do we become secure and sufficient, free from the control of circumstances and people as God intended for us to be?

In Paul's day, certain philosophers known as Stoics claimed to have learned the secret of being content. They taught that if a person eliminated all emotions, feelings, and desires by strength of will, then one would be content. In other words, no matter what happened to them, the Stoics' response was, "I don't care." As this response of not caring spread to greater and greater matters in their lives, they eventually were completely unmoved by any event or person.

While it is certainly possible to exercise one's will in this way, we might well ask, "Who wants that kind of contentment?" Indeed, who does? Someone who has willfully removed all emotional response from life is no more than a robot.

None of us want to rid ourselves of our emotions, and in fact God does not want us to live that way either. He is the One who created our capacity for emotional response. The apostle Paul was definitely not an unemotional person, as his letters to the churches make clear. He rejoiced with them, sorrowed over them, had compassion on them, and was concerned about their progress in the faith. If Paul could be content with his emotions intact, then we can too.

## LEARNING CONTENTMENT: THE FIRST STEP

So then, how do we go about learning the kind of contentment that Paul had, the kind of contentment that God wants all of His children to experience? First, *true contentment is learned by meditation*. By meditation I do not mean the practice of many Eastern religions, in which a person empties one's mind and seeks "the god within." As believers, we meditate by filling our minds with the Word of God and seeking the one true God.

Psalm 1:1–2 says, "Blessed is the man . . . [whose] delight is in the law of the LORD, and in His law he meditates day and night." When difficulties arise, we must practice turning our thoughts to the truths that God has revealed to us in His Word. The writer of Hebrews demonstrated this very thing when he wrote, "Make sure that your character is free from the love of money, being content with what you have; for He Himself has said, 'I will never desert you, nor will I ever forsake you,' so that we confidently say, 'The LORD is my helper, I will not be afraid. What will man do to me?'" (13:5–6). When we are faced with the temptation to be too concerned about money and not content with our financial situation, the writer of Hebrews urges us to do some meditating. He even provides some verses for us to think about. The first verse, "I will never desert you, nor will I ever forsake you," is a promise from Joshua 1:5 and reminds us that God is our true Provider and can take care of us regardless of how big or small our bank account happens to be. The second verse, "The LORD is my helper, I will not be afraid. What will man do to me?" is found in Psalm 118:6 and reminds us what our response should be. If God has promised to take care of us, we have no reason for concern or fear about money.

As we learn to be content through meditation, it is important that we *meditate on God's promises*. When our minds are filled with His promises, those truths will control our thoughts and responses. His promises will immediately come to mind when difficulties arise, and they will direct us to respond properly. Sadly, in today's world, meditation on the

Word of God is virtually a lost art among believers because we are constantly bombarded and distracted by the secular media, but we must discipline ourselves to make use of this important skill.

In addition to meditating on God's promises, we need to *meditate on His character* as well. We need to spend time thinking about His faithfulness, love, power, wisdom, justice, holiness, goodness, and truth. By extension, we need to also think about *our relationship* to the Father. If we are constantly thinking about the fact that God loves us far too much to do anything to us that is unkind and that He is far too wise to do anything that is foolish, we will be content. The lives of all God's children are in His loving and wise hands.

We need to also meditate on the fact that *God has a purpose for everything* that happens to us. In every situation, God is in control. Psalm 37:23 assures us, "The steps of a man are established by the LORD, and He delights in his way." Paul wrote his epistle to the Philippians from prison. We know from his letter that instead of feeling sorry for himself and despairing, Paul spent his time witnessing to the guards and encouraging the churches (1:12–14). God had important work for him to do in prison, and Paul was faithful to do it.

God can use difficult circumstances, or even what we might consider tragedies, to bring about victories for His kingdom. The crucifixion seemed a terrible tragedy to Christ's followers and disciples, but we know that it was in fact the greatest triumph because God raised Him from the dead. The early church in Jerusalem certainly did not welcome the persecution that they experienced (Acts 8), but we know now that it was God's means of getting His people out into the world so that the gospel would be spread far and wide to both Jew and Gentile.

Finally, we must meditate on the fact that *no earthly event, however great or small, in the life of one of God's children is ever the end of his existence.* We must reflect on the fact that we have a great future ahead of us. We are going to live forever, and the best is yet to come. This world is not our home. We're not home yet. Paul wrote, "The free gift of God is eternal life in Christ Jesus our Lord" (Rom. 6:23). Whatever happens to us, even death, is no more than a short, quickly passing moment in the span of eternity. As we meditate on truths such as these—God's promises, character, purposes, and the scope of eternity—we will be more content and sufficient in Christ.

## LEARNING CONTENTMENT: THE SECOND STEP

Second, *true contentment is learned by supplication.* Proverbs 18:10 teaches, "The name of the LORD is a strong tower; the righteous runs into it and is safe." David wrote, "This poor man cried, and the LORD heard him and saved him out of all his troubles" (Ps. 34:6). When we are tempted to be discontent, we must learn to seek God in prayer.

Psalm 57:1 says, "For my soul takes refuge in You; and in the shadow of Your wings I will take refuge until destruction passes by." I grew up on a farm, and David's illustration beautifully describes what happens to a flock of chickens when a dog or other supposed danger approaches. As soon as the dog appears, all the little chicks immediately scramble toward their mother. The hen quickly opens her wings and gathers her babies to her side. Likewise, when danger approaches in our lives, our first response should be to run to God for refuge.

Sir Wilfred Grenfell was a missionary doctor who at the end of the nineteenth century ministered in Labrador. On one occasion, he heard that someone needed medical help quite a distance away from where he was at the time. He quickly set out across the frozen terrain with his dogsled team. At one point during the trip, Grenfell looked back behind him and discovered that the large slab of ice over which he was traveling had broken loose. He realized that he was now floating free of the mainland, with no way of moving either back to where he started or forward to where he was going.

Not knowing quite what to do, Grenfell committed his situation to God, lay down, and went to sleep. By God's grace he was rescued a short time later. His rescuers were amazed and asked him how he could sleep while his life was in such great peril. He told them that he had committed himself to God, so there was nothing for him to fear. The knowledge that God was in control allowed him to experience complete contentment in the midst of a very difficult situation.

I firmly believe that many Christians do not experience contentment as they should because they do not take advantage of these two wonderful means of grace: meditation and supplication. In some respects, it may seem "simple" to us to think about God's truth and pray to Him in times of trouble, but such "simple" things are not often practiced. In fact, they are not simple at all, do not come naturally to us, and require a great deal of discipline. Paul wrote that he had *learned* to be content because he had *disciplined* himself for the purpose of godliness (1 Tim. 4:7).

Third, *true contentment is learned by union and communion with Jesus Christ.* Paul said, "I can do all things through Him who strengthens me" (Phil. 4:13). This verse is often quoted out of context, but it has wonderful meaning in the context of Paul's teaching on the subject of contentment. Paul was saying that he was content, ready for anything and everything, and sufficient in all situations because *Jesus* gave him the strength.

Paul was united to Jesus Christ, who is all-sufficient, and therefore Paul was sufficient through Christ's sufficiency. Another translation of Philippians 4:13 says it this way: "I am sufficient, I am strong through all things, in Him who infuses strength into me." Indeed, being a Christian means not only following the teaching and example of Christ, but also being related to Christ in such a way that His very might and power flow into and through us. "Christ in you, the hope of glory," Paul said in Colossians 1:27.

Someone once asked Martin Luther to define a Christian. He replied, "A Christian is a person in whom Jesus Christ dwells." In other words, if the life and power of Jesus Christ are not active in our lives, then we have good reason to believe that we are not His children. On the other hand, if we have committed ourselves to Christ and daily experience His power and life within us, then we are His children.

If the latter is true of us—Christ is in us and is our power and sufficiency—then we have the ability to be content. Personal willpower will never bring about true contentment. The only means by which we will ever experience true contentment in our lives is by union with Christ because His sufficiency becomes our sufficiency. Ephesians 6:10 commands, "Finally, be strong in the Lord and in the strength of His might."

Union with Christ in salvation is the only means by which we can receive the power to be content, but union with Christ is just the beginning. It is not enough only to be united to Christ in faith; we must also be in constant communion with Him. Jesus said, "I am the vine, you are the branches; he who abides in Me and I in him, he bears much fruit, for apart from Me you can do nothing" (John 15:5). In order to bear the fruit of contentment in our lives, we must abide in Christ.

What does it mean for a Christian to abide in Christ? It means that we trust Him moment by moment, day by day. It means that we meditate on Him constantly. It means that we strive after obedience to His commands at all times and in every situation. It means that we seek diligently to know Jesus better by reading and studying His Word.

One of the best ways to learn more about Christ is to study the Gospels. We can learn about Christ in all of the Word of God, but Jesus Christ is most prominent in the four Gospel accounts of Matthew, Mark, Luke, and John. I believe that all Christians should dedicate themselves to studying these books, reading them many times over, and meditating on them.

This is so profitable because the Gospels reveal in great detail the character of Christ. They also reveal how He acted and responded in all kinds of life situations. They tell us how Christ taught and trained His disciples to be content in and sufficient for all things. By carefully studying Christ's life on earth, His mind and deeds and teachings will become a part of our minds and deeds as well. This is what it means to *abide in Christ.*

If we discipline ourselves in this way, then we will not have to stop to think, "What would Jesus do?" because we will already know. The Bible teaches that Jesus was "tempted in all things as we are, yet without sin" (Heb. 4:15). If we take time to study how Jesus responded to the difficulties that He encountered in His life and ministry, then we will know what to do in similar situations.

After we have meditated on the life of Christ, we can then turn to Him in prayer, asking for help and thanking Him for the power and grace that He has promised to give us in our time of need. Once we have prepared our hearts and minds by meditation and supplication, we will be free to get up and move out in faith, believing in and expecting His help according to our need. This is what it means to abide in Christ in a practical way, and this is the "secret" to true contentment.

## APPLYING THE TRUTH

Let's consider some practical examples of how this might work in our lives. If we find ourselves afflicted by sickness or pain of some kind, we can meditate on the fact that Jesus had great compassion on the sick and hurting people that He met during His time of ministry. "When He went ashore, He saw a large crowd, and felt compassion for them and healed their sick" (Matt. 14:14). We can also meditate on His response to Paul when Paul asked to be relieved of the thorn in his flesh: "My grace is sufficient for you, for power is perfected in weakness" (2 Cor. 12:9).

Having meditated on Christ's compassion and sufficiency, we can turn to Christ in prayer and ask for His help and healing. Once we have prayed, we must then believe that Jesus will be faithful to help us as He promised. We will not know exactly how, or when, or what He will do, but we must trust with all our heart that He will do whatever brings Him glory and is best for us (Rom. 8:28). By handling a difficulty with our health in this way, we are learning to be content.

If we are being mistreated, misunderstood, or ridiculed by others, we can meditate on the many times when Jesus experienced the same thing. Men insulted Him, calling Him a drunkard and a glutton (Luke 7:34). The Pharisees tried to set traps for Him (Matt. 22:15–16). At the end of His life, He was insulted, falsely accused, beaten, and crucified.

Through all of this mistreatment, ridicule, and abuse, Christ never returned insult for insult. As Isaiah prophesied, "He was oppressed and He was afflicted, yet He did not open His mouth" (53:7). First Peter 2:21–23 also reminds us: "For you have been called for this purpose, since Christ also suffered for you, leaving you an example for you to follow in His steps, Who committed no sin, nor was any deceit found in His mouth; and while being reviled, *He did not revile in return*; while suffering, He uttered no threats, but kept entrusting Himself to Him who judges righteously." More than that, He demonstrated a readiness to forgive those who mistreated Him as He prayed, "Father, forgive them; for they do not know what they are doing" (Luke 23:34).

After we have meditated on Christ's response to mistreatment and abuse, we can pray to God for help in following His example. We can ask the Lord to give us the power to live as Jesus lived and to love as Jesus loved. Once we have meditated and prayed to God for help, we can then go on in the strength of the Lord, confident that we will receive all the help that we need to continue walking in obedience.

If we are faced with financial problems, we can meditate on Jesus' ability to turn five loaves of bread and two fishes into a feast for five thousand (Matt. 14). We can meditate on what Jesus said about not worrying about clothes or food: "Your heavenly Father knows that you need all these things. But seek first His kingdom and His righteousness, and all these things will be added to you" (Matt. 6:32–33). We can turn to God in prayer, asking Him to provide for our needs as He promised and was faithful to do for His disciples.

If we are dealing with the death of a loved one or our own approaching death, we can meditate on Jesus' sorrow and compassion on the occasion of the death of Lazarus. We can think about how He spoke to the synagogue official's daughter and raised her up (Mark 5) and how He experienced death Himself. We can meditate on Christ's promise in John 11:25–26, "I am the resurrection and the life; he who believes in Me will live even if he dies, and everyone who lives and believes in Me will never die." Knowing these things, we can pray for help and rest on the promise that we will receive that help.

If we are struggling with sin and guilt in our life, we can think about how Jesus forgave the woman who was living in adultery and who had had five husbands (John 4). We can think about the compassion He had for the adulterous woman who was about to be stoned. He rebuked her accusers and then forgave her: "I do not condemn you, either. Go. From now on sin no more" (John 8:11).

We can also remember how Jesus spoke to Zaccheus, ate with him, and granted salvation to him (Luke 19), and what He said to the scribes of the Pharisees, "I did not come to call the righteous, but sinners" (Mark 2:17). Then we can turn to God in prayer, asking for forgiveness and help in resisting temptation, knowing that He will give it because "God demonstrates His own love toward us, in that while we were yet sinners, Christ died for us" (Rom. 5:8).

Oliver Cromwell was a great man of history and also a great man of God. After the death of his son, Cromwell fell into despair and wondered if life was worth living. During this dark time in his life, he came across Philippians 4:13, "I can do all things through Him who strengthens me." Meditating on and clinging to the truth in that verse helped him to overcome this difficult circumstance. Later in his life, he would often point out that verse to others, saying, "Mister, that verse saved my life!"

Cromwell was not finished learning about contentment, however. Sometime later, his daughter also died. As he sat with a group of friends in his home, he asked for a Bible and read to them Philippians 4:11–12: "Not that I speak from want, for I have learned to be content in whatever circumstance I am. I know how to get along with humble means, and I also know how to live in prosperity; in any and every circumstance I have learned the secret of being filled and going hungry, both of having abundance and suffering need." Cromwell then said, "It is a hard thing to learn contentment in circumstances like these. How can I learn contentment? *I can do all things through Christ who strengthens me.*"

The Lord Jesus Christ gave Paul the power to be content in every circumstance. Paul received this power as he meditated on Christ, prayed to Him, and lived in union and communion with Him. Oliver Cromwell received this power also when he studied God's words through the apostle Paul and learned the "secret" of being content. As believers, we all can have the power to be content as well. If we meditate on our Lord Jesus Christ, pray to Him, and abide in Him, we can and we will "overwhelmingly conquer through Him who loved us" (Rom. 8:37)!

## APPLICATION

1. Considering the kind of life Paul had and what he was able to say about the level of contentment in his life, how would you rate the level of contentment in your life right now, on a scale of 1 to 5 (1 = very discontented, 5 = always content)?

2. Write out Philippians 4:13. Do you really believe this is true? Why or why not?

3. When Paul said that he was always "content," what did he mean? What is true contentment?

4. Can a person be truly content and still work for change in life and in the world? How do these two things work together?

5. Write out 2 Peter 1:3. How does this verse apply to being truly content?

6. What does the fact that we must *learn* to be content mean for your life right now?

7. Why is the Stoic's approach to contentment wrong?

8. What is the first step to learning true contentment?

9. What does it mean for a Christian to meditate?

10. How did the writer of Hebrews demonstrate using meditation when facing difficulty?

11. How does meditation help us become more content?

12. What are four major things that we should meditate on to increase our contentment?

13. Write down two or three verses from this chapter that impacted you the most. Work on memorizing them.

14. What is the second step to learning true contentment?

15. What image did David use to illustrate how he turned to God in prayer during difficult circumstances?

16. In what ways do you need to become more disciplined in meditation and in prayer?

17. Why are meditation and prayer so difficult to actually do?

18. What is the only means by which we are able to be truly content (Phil. 4:13)?

19. What does it mean to be united to Christ?

20. How does being united to Christ make us able to be content?

21. Why are the Gospels such a valuable resource in helping us to abide in Christ?

22. Do you agree with the message of this chapter—that true contentment comes only through Jesus Christ and that it is possible for you to experience it if you are willing to learn? If so, why? If not, why not?

23. In what ways have you failed to be content in the past (be specific)?

24. In what aspects of your life right now do you need to learn contentment?

25. What truths from God's Word can you meditate on to help you learn to be content in these aspects of your life? Find three or four passages for each area you identify.

26. What can you do to help you to meditate and remember to meditate on these truths? Be specific.

27. What practical things can you do to improve your communion with Jesus Christ on a daily basis?

# 10

# PERPLEXITY
# AND CONFUSION

There are times in every Christian's life when the path becomes obscured by darkness and it is quite difficult, if not impossible, to discern the reason or the cure. Like others, I have faced this problem many times and have found a certain verse in Isaiah to be most instructive. I use it often in my counseling as I work with people who are in the midst of hard times and do not know what to do. Isaiah 50:10 says, "Who is among you that fears the LORD, that obeys the voice of His servant, that walks in darkness and has no light? Let him trust in the name of the LORD and rely on his God."

This verse begins with a question and then gives some directions. As I have studied this verse, I have come to focus on three particular things in it: one, the identity of the people to whom the verse is addressed; two, the problem that these people have; and three, God's direction for handling this problem. I believe that as we study these three things together, God's solution for this problem will become clear.

## WHO ARE THE PEOPLE WHO WALK IN DARKNESS?

First, we need to consider the fact that the words of this verse are addressed to people with two important characteristics. One, they are people who *fear God*: "Who is among you that fears the LORD?" This is significant because when the Bible says that someone fears the Lord, it means that he or she is a child of God. In fact, a lack of fear of God is used to describe people who do not know Christ—who are not believers. For example, Psalm 36:1 says, "Transgression speaks to the ungodly within his heart; there is no fear of God before his eyes." Romans 3:18 teaches that our world is full of ungodliness and ungodly people because there is no fear of God. On the other hand, when the Scripture describes believers, it says that they fear God. In Deuteronomy 10:12 God gave Israel some requirements for being His people: "Now, Israel, what does the LORD your God require from you, but to fear the LORD your God, to walk in all His ways and love Him, and to serve the LORD your God with all your heart and with all your soul . . . ?" As a professor at The Master's College, I always gave my students a list of requirements for passing my courses. If a student wanted to pass the course, he or she absolutely had to complete the items on that list. God's requirements for His people begin with fearing Him.

The fear of God as a characteristic of believers is mentioned over and over in Scripture. God's servant is thus described in Job 1:1: "There was a man in the land of Uz whose name was Job; and that man was blameless, upright, *fearing God* and turning away from evil." Ecclesiastes 12:13 summarizes: "The conclusion, when all has been heard, is: fear God and keep His commandments, because this applies to every person." In Jeremiah 32:38–40 God spoke about those He was going to save: "They shall be My people, and I will be their God; and I will give them one heart and one way, that they may fear Me always, for their own good and for the good of their children after them. I will make an everlasting covenant with them that I will not turn away from them, to do them good; and I will put the fear of Me in their hearts so that they will not turn away from Me."

In Matthew 10:28 Jesus emphasized the importance of fearing God: "Do not fear those who kill the body but are unable to kill the soul; but rather fear Him who is able to destroy both soul and body in hell." One of the characteristics of the believers in the early church was that they were "going on in the fear of the Lord" (Acts 9:31). Paul taught us to "be subject to one another in the fear of Christ" (Eph. 5:21) and to "work out your salvation with fear and trembling" (Phil. 2:12). Peter exhorted us, if we call God our Father, to "conduct [ourselves] in fear" (1 Peter 1:17).

Clearly, the fear of the Lord is essential to saving faith and a distinguishing mark of a true believer. Since the fear of the Lord is so important, we must then answer this question: What does it mean to "fear" the Lord? Though we commonly use the word "fear" to mean being scared or frightened of something, this is not the way the Bible uses the word "fear" when it is speaking about the attitude toward God that all believers must have.

The words used for this kind of fear are the Hebrew word *yārō'* and the Greek word *phobeō*, both of which mean "to reverence" or "to be in awe of." A person who "fears the Lord" is someone who reverences, respects, serves, and loves God. Hebrews 12:28 enjoins, "Therefore, since we receive a kingdom which cannot be shaken, let us show gratitude, by which we may offer to God an acceptable service with reverence and awe." We already noted Deuteronomy 10:12, which connects the fear of God to obeying Him, loving Him, and serving Him.

Scripture also indicates that a person who fears God is serious about spiritual matters. Psalm 2:11 says, "Worship the Lord with reverence and rejoice with trembling." In other words, true believers do not come into God's presence giggling and carrying on; they come with great reverence and respect because they recognize the awesome glory of God. In fact, we learn in Scripture that those who found themselves in the presence of God and saw something of His glory reacted accordingly with great fear and trembling.

Scripture also teaches that people who fear God are God-centered in all areas of their life. They are not like the ungodly person described in Psalm 10:4: "The wicked, in the haughtiness of his countenance, does not seek Him." In contrast, the godly live according to Proverbs 3:5–7, "Trust in the Lord with all your heart and do not lean on your own understanding. In all your ways acknowledge Him, and he will make your paths straight. Do not be wise in your own eyes; fear the Lord and turn away from evil." A godly person has the Lord in his thoughts always, about everything—family, business, time, money, relationships. There is no part of his life where God is not the focus.

Paul was a God-fearing man whose sole ambition in life was to exalt God through obedience to Him. In Philippians 1:20–21 Paul said, "Christ will even now, as always, be exalted in my body, whether by life or by death. For to me, to live is Christ." In 2 Corinthians 5:9–11 he said, "Therefore we also have as our ambition . . . to be pleasing to Him. . . . Therefore, knowing the fear of the Lord, we persuade men, but we are made manifest to God." Paul was a God-fearing man whose only purpose in life was to exalt Christ.

Ultimately, people who fear God do so because they believe God. They believe what God has revealed in His Word about their innate sinfulness, their inability to please God by themselves, their need for forgiveness, and their need for a Savior. They believe that only God can save them and make them a new creature in Christ through the renewing of the Holy Spirit. They believe all these things because "The fear of the LORD is the beginning of wisdom, and the knowledge of the Holy One is understanding" (Prov. 9:10).

Fearing the Lord is the first characteristic of the people to whom Isaiah 50:10 was addressed. The second characteristic of these people is that they *obey God*—"that obeys the voice of His servant"—because obedience is a natural consequence of true fear. The "servant" that this verse refers to is the Lord Jesus Christ. In the book of Isaiah, chapters 40–66 refer to the servant of Jehovah, who is Christ. Isaiah 52:13 speaks of "My servant" and is then followed by Isaiah 53, which describes the crucifixion of Christ.

In fact, Jesus acknowledged His role as the servant of God many times while on earth. In John 4:34 He said, "My food is to do the will of Him who sent Me and to accomplish His work." Just before going to the cross, Christ said, "I glorified You on the earth, having accomplished the work which You have given Me to do" (John 17:4). He constantly taught His disciples to do the same, most notably in John 13 when He washed the disciples' feet and instructed them: "If I then, the Lord and the Teacher, washed your feet, you also ought to wash one another's feet. For I gave you an example that you also should do as I did to you" (13:14–15).

Just as Jesus obeyed God completely, those who desire to be His disciples must obey God completely. The Bible says that Job "was blameless, upright, fearing God and turning away from evil" (1:1). In other words, he obeyed God. Proverbs 8:13 teaches, "The fear of the LORD is to hate evil." Those who hate evil will love righteousness, and loving righteousness means living in obedience to God.

We see then that Isaiah 50:10 is clearly addressed to people who are true believers—who fear the Lord and obey Christ; however, these people have a serious problem. According to Isaiah, they "walk in darkness and have no light." To understand what God meant by the words "walk in darkness," we need to consider the meaning of the word "darkness" in this context.

## WHAT WALKING IN DARKNESS MEANS

Sometimes "darkness" is used as a synonym for "sin," as in John 3:19, "men loved the darkness rather than the Light, for their deeds were evil," and Ephesians 5:11, "Do not participate in the unfruitful deeds of darkness, but instead even expose them." In Isaiah 50:10, however, the word "darkness" is clearly not used to mean "sin." If people fear the Lord and obey Christ, then they cannot also be described as walking in sin.

Another meaning of the word "darkness" in Scripture is "a lack of understanding or insight," and this is the way that the word is being used in Isaiah 50:10. The word is used in the same way in Ephesians 4:18, which speaks of people "being darkened in their understanding." And 2 Corinthians 4:6 says, "For God, who said, 'Light shall shine out of darkness,' is the One who has shone in our hearts to give the Light of the knowledge of the glory of God in the face of Christ."

Before I came to Christ at age sixteen, I did not know God or the Word of God. I was not interested in spiritual things, in submitting to Jesus as my Lord, or in worshipping God. Though I went to church every Sunday and was outwardly religious, my heart was far from God. When God changed my heart, the darkness vanished before the Light, and my whole life was changed. This happened, though, only because God gave me knowledge—knowledge of Himself, of myself, of salvation, and of how to live in obedience to Him.

All the same, though I am a true believer, I still experience times in my life in which I am walking in darkness about certain matters and have no light. Psalm 82:5 says of this kind of situation, "They do not know nor do they understand; they walk about in darkness; all the foundations of the earth are shaken." These are times when we are unable to discern the specific purposes of the Lord in our circumstances or the circumstances of those around us.

This darkness is also described in Psalm 44. In verses 4–8 the psalmist praises and thanks God for victory over and deliverance from enemies. He reveals that he has been walking in fear and obedience: "For I will not trust in my bow," and "In God we have boasted all day long." However, in verse 9 he continues, "Yet You have rejected us and brought us to dishonor, and do not go out with our armies." He goes on to describe all the ways that he had experienced dishonor, disappointment, and defeat: "You make us a reproach to our neighbors, a scoffing and a derision to those around us" (v. 13), and yet he notes: "All this had come upon us, but we have not forgotten You, and we have not dealt falsely with Your covenant. Our heart has not turned back, and our steps have not deviated from Your way" (vv. 17–18).

In other words, this man who was walking in fear of and obedience to the Lord was going through a period of darkness in which he was not able to discern the purposes of God. He wrote in this psalm that he did not understand why he and those around him were experiencing difficulties. This kind of darkness occurs in the lives of most believers from time to time. John Bunyan describes the experience in his insightful book on the Christian life, *The Pilgrim's Progress.* At one point in this book, Christian goes through the Valley of the Shadow, which is described as a lonely place, a wilderness filled with deserts and pits and the shadow of death, a land of drought, and a place of pitch darkness. In this dreadful, chaotic place, believers experience much confusion. This is the "darkness" to which Isaiah was referring.

When believers go through such a time in their lives, when they walk in darkness and have no light, they are in great danger because in such times they are tempted to respond sinfully to their circumstances. In Bunyan's tale, as Christian walked through the Valley of the Shadow, the path on which he walked was very narrow. It would have been easy for him to fall on either side, with a ditch on his right and a bottomless quagmire on his left.

The ditch on Christian's right represented false teaching and counsel. In Matthew 15:14 Jesus said, "And if a blind man guides a blind man, both will fall into a pit." He was referring to the false teachings of the Pharisees, Sadducees, and scribes when He said this, as Bunyan illustrated beautifully in his tale. When we are in a place of darkness—faced with a situation that we do not understand—we are most susceptible to the pseudounderstanding of unbiblical counselors because we crave answers.

Indeed, no one likes to walk in darkness. On the contrary, we naturally seek meaning and reason in our lives. It can be very difficult to walk long in difficult circumstances without being able to understand their meaning. Sadly, the world around us is rich in false counsel—on the radio, in self-help books, in magazines, and on television. If we are not careful, blind teachers will quickly lead us off the path and we will fall into the ditch with them. Whatever is not based on the Scripture from first to last is false teaching and will lead us astray.

The bottomless quagmire on Christian's left was a deep swamp that represented great insecurity, despair, depression, and hopelessness. Sometimes when we are facing difficulties that we do not understand, we are tempted to become depressed and discouraged. We feel like the writer of Psalm 73: "But as for me, my feet came close to stumbling, my steps had almost slipped. . . . Surely in vain I have kept my heart pure and washed my hands in innocence; for I have been stricken all day long and chastened every morning" (73:2, 13–14).

Another danger of the quagmire is sinking into sinful pleasures. During a time of darkness, when the Christian life is no longer a source of joy, believers are tempted to find happiness and peace in sins such as drugs, alcohol, or sexual promiscuity. These things provide a small amount of temporary relief and pleasure, but are in fact a quagmire. They drag people away from the path of godliness, can be very hard to let go of, and always leave the person who indulged in them in worse shape than before, despite whatever temporary enjoyment they provided.

## WHAT TO DO WHEN YOU WALK IN DARKNESS

It is a serious problem to be faced with these kinds of temptations—the ditch of false teaching and the quagmire of depression and sinful pleasures—when experiencing a time of darkness, but God, as He always does, has a solution to our problem. Isaiah 50:10 says, "Let him trust in the name of the LORD and rely on his God." In order to fully appreciate the solution provided in this verse, we must consider two aspects of it carefully.

First, the phrase "Let him trust" means that we need to make a conscious decision about the attitude of our hearts, as David did in Psalm 56:3–4: "When I am afraid, I will put my trust in You. In God, whose word I praise, in God I have put my trust; I shall not be afraid. What can mere man do to me?"

David made a commitment in his heart about what he would do when faced with fear or discouragement; we must do the same. As believers, we can never allow ourselves to be passive because passive hearts and minds quickly forget the truth and stop trusting. The Christian life must be lived proactively if it is to be lived successfully.

Second, when the Bible uses the phrase "in the name of the LORD," it is referring to the meaning of God's name— what it reveals about His character, not the name itself. To trust in the name of the Lord is to trust in the Lord Himself and all that His name declares Him to be. For example, one of the names of God is "Jehovah," which means "eternal." In Exodus 3:14 God revealed Himself to Moses as "I AM WHO I AM." Jehovah God is unchangeable; He is the same yesterday, today, and forever. The name Jehovah emphasizes the fact that God is faithful; He keeps His covenants with and promises to His people because He never changes.

The Scripture also reveals that God is the "Almighty God" (Gen. 17:1). When we trust in the Lord God Almighty, we are trusting in a God who is absolutely sovereign. The Scripture is full of testimony to the sovereignty of God. Psalm 115:3 says, "But our God is in the heavens; He does whatever He pleases." Jeremiah 32:17 declares, "Ah Lord GOD! Behold, You have made the heavens and the earth by Your great power and by Your outstretched arm! Nothing is too difficult for You." In Daniel 4:35 Nebuchadnezzar acknowledged, "But He does according to His will in the host of heaven and among the inhabitants of earth; and no one can ward off His hand or say to Him, 'What have You done?' " In Matthew 19:26 Jesus taught, "with God all things are possible." And Ephesians 3:20 ascribes glory "to Him who is able to do far more abundantly beyond all that we ask or think, according to the power that works within us."

"Jehovah" and "Almighty God" are just two of God's names; there are many, many more. Each name reveals specific things about the character of God, and when we are walking in darkness, we need to fill our minds with the names of God and meditate on their meanings. We need to remember that God is eternal (unchangeable), omnipotent (all-powerful), omniscient (all-knowing), and all-wise. Whatever He allows in our lives is according to His infinite wisdom, faithfulness, and lovingkindness.

If we trust in human wisdom when walking in darkness, whether our own or other people's wisdom, instead of trusting in God, we will fall into the ditch or the quagmire. The only way safely through the darkness is to commit our hearts to trusting solely in the wisdom of God and in His character as it is revealed in the Scripture and in the Lord Jesus Christ. In other words, we must not look at God through our circumstances, but rather we must look at our circumstances through God.

This is what the disciples failed to do in Mark 4 when they were frightened by the storm. They looked at the wind and the waves (their circumstances), and when they saw Jesus sleeping in the back of the boat, they assumed that He did not care what happened to them: they looked at Jesus through their circumstances. Jesus had to rebuke them for their lack of faith—their inability to trust in His love for them and His power to save them—and for judging Him on the basis of what they saw happening and what they thought His response should be to their circumstances.

This is precisely what we are often tempted to do in times of darkness, and this is also what God is teaching us in Isaiah 50:10 *not* to do. If we see the storm and feel that God is not doing what we think He should be doing, we will become frightened and stop trusting, or having faith, in Him. The solution, God says, is to trust. In other words, we must take ourselves by the scruff of the neck, so to speak, and resolve in our hearts to rely on God.

Since God has revealed Himself to us in His Word, we must spend time meditating on the Word of God so that we are better able to trust in Him. The Scripture is an invaluable resource for reminding us of the things we need to know in order to put our trust in God: His character, His promises, and our need for Him. In times of darkness we need the light of God's Word. As David said in Psalm 56:3–4, I will put my trust in You. In God, whose word I praise, in God I have put my trust."

The life of John Bunyan is an excellent example of someone filling his mind with the Word of God during a time of great difficulty and darkness. Bunyan spent twelve and half years in prison because he refused to stop preaching the Word of God. During that time he studied the Word of God intensively and filled some forty books with the insight that God gave him, one of which was the masterful work *The Pilgrim's Progress*. Despite the fact that he was in prison for twelve and half years—apart from his family and children and unable to support them in any way—his mind was so filled with the Word of God that he never fell into the ditch of false teaching or the quagmire of depression. Charles Spurgeon once said that Bunyan was so filled with the Word of God that if someone had pricked him, "his blood would have flowed bibline."

All believers should strive for such intimate knowledge of the Word of God that they are able to evaluate every situation of life with the wisdom of God. Paul urged, "Let the word of Christ richly dwell within you, with all wisdom teaching and admonishing one another . . ." (Col. 3:16). For such a person, the Scripture becomes the standard by which all else is measured, and when measured by this standard, all things are evaluated correctly.

There will be times of darkness—of this we can be sure. We will not always, or perhaps often, be able to figure out the mind of God; indeed, He is God and we are not. Our mind is like a small teacup that cannot begin to hold the ocean of God's wisdom and understanding. One of my seminary professors liked to say, "Let's let God know some things that we don't know." Truly, instead of despairing in the darkness, discouraged by our lack of knowledge, we must learn to trust and rely on God because His wisdom is infinite.

Yes, "our God is in the heavens; He does whatever He pleases" (Ps. 115:3), but He demonstrates His love, wisdom, and faithfulness by working all things together for our good (Rom. 8:28). Job, a man who feared and obeyed God, went through a time of great darkness, but the Scripture does not reveal that God ever explained to Job the reason for that darkness, though Job certainly wanted to know.

For some twenty chapters of the book of Job, Job asks God for an answer. God does not give him the answer that he wants, but He does give the only answer that Job needs:

Then the LORD answered Job out of the whirlwind
      and said,
*"Who is this that darkens counsel*
*By words without knowledge?*
Now gird up your loins like a man,
And I will ask you, and you instruct Me!" (Job 38:1–3)

Then the LORD said to Job,
"Will the faultfinder contend with the Almighty?
Let him who reproves God answer it."

Then Job answered the LORD and said,
"Behold, I am insignificant; what can I reply to You?
I lay my hand on my mouth.
Once I have spoken, and I will not answer;
Even twice, and I will add nothing more."

Then the LORD answered Job out of the storm and
      said,
"Now gird up your loins like a man;
I will ask you, and you instruct Me.
Will you really annul My judgment?
Will you condemn Me that you may be justified?
Or do you have an arm like God?
And can you thunder with a voice like His?" (40:1–9)

Then Job answered the LORD and said,
"I know that You can do all things,
And that no purpose of Yours can be thwarted.
'Who is this that hides counsel without knowledge?'
*Therefore I have declared that which I did not understand,*

*Things too wonderful for me, which I did not know."*
(42:1–3)

Job eventually learned what we must learn as well: that God is God and we are not. The only way to not succumb to temptation in times of darkness is to learn to trust. When Job was tempted to despair from his lack of understanding, God stepped in and forced him to think about His greatness. God reminded Job of His awesome power, His love, His wisdom, and His holiness. He reminded Job of his insignificance so that Job would realize that his only hope was to entrust himself to the Almighty God.

In Isaiah 50:10 God reminds us to do the same when we are walking in darkness: "Who is among you that fears the LORD, that obeys the voice of His servant, that walks in darkness and has no light? Let him trust in the name of the LORD and rely on his God." If we are serious about overcoming the darkness, we must commit ourselves to living in fear and obedience every day and to trusting in God at all times.

We must also commit ourselves to training our minds to dwell on God's wisdom by learning, studying, and meditating on the Word of God. God has promised that His Word will be a lamp to our feet and a light to our path (Ps. 119:105). David said, "In Your light we see light" (Ps. 36:9). That light is the Lord Jesus, who is revealed to us by the Word of God. May God help us to find the solution to our problem of not knowing what to do by trusting in the name of the Lord and relying on our God.

In God I have put my trust;
I shall not be afraid.

What can man do to me? . . .
For You have delivered my soul from death,
Indeed my feet from stumbling,
So that I may walk before God
In the light of the living. (Ps. 56:11, 13)

## APPLICATION

1. This chapter is based on Isaiah 50:10. Write out this verse and include it as one of the verses you will work on memorizing.

2. Identify and describe the people to whom this verse is addressed. What are their general characteristics?

3. In specific terms, what does it mean to fear God? List some of the things mentioned in this chapter that characterize the person who fears God.

4. As you compare your life to the characteristics of a person who fears God that are mentioned in this chapter, how would you rate your fear of God? Use the following rating scale: 4 = excellent (usually true of me); 3 = good (often true of me); 2 = somewhat and sometimes true of me (needs much improvement); 1 = very lacking and seldom true of me (needs very much improvement); 0 = never true of me.

5. Using the specific characteristics of a God-fearing person described in this chapter as your guide, write out the specific ways in which you need to improve.

6. When Isaiah 50:10 mentions "walking in darkness," what experience is it referring to?

7. Why is "walking in darkness" a dangerous time for people?

8. What two dangers are people prone to fall into when they "walk in darkness"?

9. Describe a "walking in darkness" that you have experienced or are experiencing. What were or are the circumstances? How did it affect you? What did you do or are you doing? What were or are you thinking and feeling?

10. What does Isaiah 50:10 tell us to do when we "walk in darkness"?

11. What does it mean to "trust in the name of the Lord"?

12. What are some of the names of the Lord (e.g., "Father") and descriptive titles (e.g., "Shepherd") that are most meaningful to you?

13. What must you do to help yourself to follow the counsel of this verse when you "walk in darkness"?

14. How can the information presented in this chapter be of practical help in your own life and in your ministry to others?

# 11

## DISCOURAGEMENT

In my experience as a biblical counselor, I sometimes encounter people who have had secular counseling for previous or current problems. Though they sometimes experience some temporary relief, it never provides a lasting, God-honoring solution. This is not a surprise because no real truth is ever given to them that could bring about lasting, God-honoring change. Sadly, there are many Christians in counseling today who either do not know or do not believe that the Bible really has all the solutions to life's problems.

The Word of God provides for us comprehensive, though not exhaustive, information regarding every problem of life and is therefore sufficient for us in all matters. Though every issue of life is not specifically addressed in detail (meaning that the Bible's coverage is not exhaustive), every issue of life *is* touched on sufficiently to give us guidance. For example, I have heard it argued that since the Bible never mentions certain problems by name, such as anorexia nervosa, we should not consider the Bible as the source of solutions to such problems. In reality, nothing could be further from the truth.

While it is certainly true that a problem such as anorexia is never *specifically* mentioned in Scripture, it is also true that the Bible contains the basic principles needed to address this problem. Proverbs 4:23 teaches that "out of [the heart] spring the issues of life" (NKJV). Though the outer symptoms of anorexia are not addressed or even mentioned in Scripture, the heart issues of a person who is struggling with anorexia are dealt with in the Word of God.

God meant for His Word to be the one and only source of solutions for man's problems. The psalmist said of Scripture, "Your commandment is exceedingly broad" (Ps. 119:96). Paul wrote of the sufficiency of God's Word, "All Scripture is inspired by God and profitable for teaching, for reproof, for correction, for training in righteousness; so that the man of God may be adequate, equipped for every good work" (2 Tim. 3:16–17).

As we have seen already, problems such as anxiety, spiritual burnout, discontentment, feeling sorry for self, perplexity, and confusion are problems that many—if not all—believers struggle with at some point in their lives. They are in every sense temptations that are "common to man," which God has promised to give us strength to endure while we are in the midst of them and to provide a way of escape out of them (1 Cor. 10:13). In the same way that careful study of the Scriptures provided God's solution to the problems discussed in former chapters, we can expect that it will provide God's solution to the common problem of discouragement as well.

Who of us has never been discouraged? It is hardly possible to live in this sin-cursed world without experiencing situations in which we are tempted to be discouraged. Some very godly men of the Bible struggled with discouragement, including Job, Moses, David, and the prophets Elijah and Jeremiah. In Psalms 42–43 the psalmist asked three times, "Why are you in despair, O my soul? And why have you become disturbed within me?" (Ps. 42:5, 11; 43:5).

When discouragement comes, it is usually experienced in connection with some distressing circumstance in which we find ourselves. It may be poor health (our own or a loved one's), ridicule or abuse by co-workers or family members, personal failure, realization of repeated sin, events in the world around us, problems in the church, or countless other problems. Whether we are experiencing events in our lives right now that could lead to discouragement or not, we may be sure that we will at some point. Jesus warned us: "In the world you have tribulation" (John 16:33).

## GOD'S SOLUTION TO DISCOURAGEMENT

There is a wonderful solution to this problem of discouragement; it is found in Jude 24–25: "Now to Him who is able to keep you from stumbling, and to make you stand in the presence of His glory blameless with great joy, to the only God our Savior, through Jesus Christ our Lord, be glory, majesty, dominion and authority, before all time and now and forever. Amen." Though many regard these verses as simply a closing doxology (a hymn of praise), I believe that they are much more than that. These two verses provide God's solution to the problem of discouragement.

Earlier in this epistle Jude described the difficult times in which the people to whom the letter was originally written were living. He warned them about ungodly individuals who had come into the church and were denying the truth, defiling their bodies, rejecting authority, and reviling angelic majesties (vv. 4–8). He warned his readers about what these people believed: "But these men revile the things which they do not understand"(v. 10). And he described how they were behaving toward others: "These are grumblers, finding fault, following after their own lusts; they speak arrogantly, flattering people for the sake of gaining an advantage" (v. 16).

Then, in verses 17–23, Jude challenged his readers to accept some very weighty responsibilities. Because of the difficulties these ungodly people brought upon the church, he commanded the church to do some hard things. He told them to remember what the apostles of Christ had taught them (v. 17), to build one another up in the faith, to pray in the Holy Spirit (v. 20), to keep themselves in the love of God, to wait anxiously for the mercy of Christ (v. 21), to have mercy on those who were doubting, and to have mercy on those who were in sin (vv. 22–23).

These instructions are followed by the marvelous doxology in verses 24 and 25, in which Jude reminds the church of three important truths: who God is, what God has, and what God can do. I believe that these truths are especially relevant in times when we find ourselves tempted to become discouraged due to difficult circumstances and great responsibilities. Let's consider each of Jude's three instructions carefully.

## Remembering Who and What God Is

First, when facing potentially discouraging circumstances, we must remember *who God is*. In verse 25 Jude wrote that God is "the only God." It is a tremendously encouraging thought to realize that our God is the *only* God that exists. This was an especially relevant truth for the early church because Greek thinking influenced so much of the world at that time. The Greeks believed in many gods: Zeus, Hera, Artemis, Apollo, and so on. In fact, this greatly angered Paul in Acts 17:16: "Now while Paul was waiting for them at Athens, his spirit was being provoked within him as he was observing the city full of idols."

Some time ago, I visited an ancient building called the Pantheon. The Greek word "pantheon" means "all gods." The Pantheon was an enormous temple full of statues to each of the gods. Besides the fact that these gods were false gods, they were also little more than elevated humans. The ancients imagined that these gods fought among themselves, were jealous of each other, and had sexual relationships with each other and with humans.

By way of contrast, Jude emphasizes the fact that, as Christians, we know that there is only *one* God. Deuteronomy 6:4 proclaims, "Hear, O Israel! The LORD is our God, the LORD is one!" Paul taught in 1 Timothy 2:5, "For there is one God, and one mediator also between God and men, the man Christ Jesus." He also wrote, "He who is the blessed and only Sovereign, the King of kings and Lord of lords, who alone possesses immortality and dwells in unapproachable light, whom no man has seen or can see" (1 Tim. 6:15–16).

It is important for us to reflect on the truth of who God is because there are many false ideas, even among believers, about who Satan is. Some people seem to think that Satan is as omniscient, omnipresent, and omnipotent as God is. In reality, Satan is none of these things; he is a created being with very limited powers that do not even begin to approach the powers of the Almighty God.

I have counseled people who were terribly frightened of Satan because of things that they had read or heard from supposedly Christian sources. While it is true that Satan and his demons are powerful beings in this world and should not be trifled with, they are in no way equal to God. Quite the contrary, they are under the complete control of God and can do only what He allows them to do. God alone "does according to His will in the host of heaven and among the inhabitants of earth" (Dan. 4:35).

When faced with potentially discouraging situations in our lives, we need to remind ourselves that no one is God but God. There is no real power in Satan or any other created things: the forces of nature, the rulers of this world, the armies and weapons of this world, diseases, or anything else. God reigns over all of these and directs them according to His will.

Not only that, but we need to remember that this one God is our Savior as well: "to the only God our Savior" (Jude 25). Some people's picture of God is of a Creator and Judge only. They imagine Him to be constantly condemning us and demanding from us far more than we could ever do. They think of Him as far away, indifferent to our needs, and capricious in handling the affairs of earth. Sadly, I have worked with many Christians who have such a view of our God.

I remember one very discouraged man I worked with who was raised in a Roman Catholic home. His mother, though very religious, was very strict with him. He received no love or affection from her. In fact, she disliked him so much that when he fell off the kitchen stool as a child and broke a bone, his mother refused to respond in any way. He had to crawl to the phone and call for an ambulance himself. Needless to say, this man came to hate his mother and because of her example hated God as well.

As a young adult, my counselee made it his ambition to prove to his mother that he was not the loser that she had called him for so many years of his childhood. He made large amounts of money doing very dangerous work and quickly became a multimillionaire. Despite his success, however, he was miserable; when he was about to commit suicide, the Lord moved him to pick up a Bible. He began reading and by God's grace was saved by the truth of the Word of God.

In the providence of God, this man joined a Bible-believing church and was referred to me by his pastor for counseling. He and his wife were having problems in their marriage because his view of God had not changed much after his salvation. He treated his wife much as his mother had treated him because, although he knew in a factual way that God was his Savior, he had not yet really embraced that truth in his heart. In our counseling together, we focused on helping him to understand what it means to have God as Savior. And in so doing, as he came to understand and embrace the relevance of this concept, his attitude and actions were changed dramatically.

Truly understanding how God is our Savior is important for us as believers because He is our Savior in so many ways. He is our Savior, first, from sin: "and you shall call His name Jesus, for He will save His people from their sins" (Matt. 1:21). God is our Savior from the penalty, the power, and (one day) the presence of our sin. Though this is indeed the most important aspect of God as our Savior, there are others as well.

God is also our Savior physically; He delivers and protects our physical bodies from harm. "For in Him we live and move and exist" (Acts 17:28). In fact, God sustains all of creation continuously and preserves it until the day that He has determined for its eventual destruction. "He is before all things, and in Him all things hold together" (Col. 1:17).

He is our Savior from our personal difficulties as well. For example, in Psalm 34 David wrote, "I sought the LORD, and He answered me, and delivered me from all my fears. . . . This poor man cried, and the LORD heard him and saved him out of all his troubles" (34:4, 6). Likewise, in Psalm 107:4–6:

> They wandered in the wilderness in a desert region;
>     they did not find a way to an inhabited city.
> They were hungry and thirsty; their soul fainted
>     within them.
> Then they cried out to the LORD in their trouble; He
>     delivered them out of their distresses.

Indeed, God wants to be our Savior in every sense: initially and most importantly from sin, but also from physical and emotional troubles. We have the privilege of living in a restored relationship with this Savior God as a result of Christ's death and resurrection. As David exulted, "The LORD is my light and my salvation; whom shall I fear? The LORD is the defense of my life; whom shall I dread?" (Ps. 27:1).

In addition to asserting that God is the only God and our Savior, Jude pointed out that God is our Savior "through Jesus Christ our Lord." In other words, God is not our Savior through the church, through our works of righteousness, through acts of penitence, through our perfection, or even through our faith—in the sense that faith is something that we bring forth of our own accord—because God *gives* us faith. He is our Savior through Jesus Christ alone. "And there is salvation in no one else; for there is no other name under heaven that has been given among men by which we must be saved" (Acts 4:12).

It is this truth that gives us assurance; if we are united to Jesus Christ, then we need never fear. "All that the Father gives Me will come to Me, and the one who comes to Me I will certainly not cast out" (John 6:37). This truth also gives us confidence, as the writer of Hebrews taught: "Therefore let us draw near with confidence to the throne of grace, so that we may receive mercy and find grace to help in time of need" (Heb. 4:16). As believers, we will certainly have times of need, but we can confidently expect that God will give us grace and mercy in those times of need because He is our Savior through Jesus Christ.

When we forget these truths and live as if they did not exist, it is then that we become discouraged. Discouragement results from not constantly thinking rightly about God.

Though most of us would agree with Jude's description of who God is, even in times of distress, we become discouraged because these truths are not foremost in our minds. How true is this wonderful chorus: "Turn your eyes upon Jesus, look full in His wonderful face. And the things of earth will grow strangely dim, in the light of His glory and grace."

There is a section in *The Pilgrim's Progress* in which a man comes through a gate (which represents Jesus Christ), but he still feels the burden of his sin. He is still discouraged and cast down. He then comes to a cross, and when he looks at the cross and understands more fully the meaning of that cross, the burden falls off his back and rolls into an empty tomb.

Some readers find this passage difficult to understand, but I believe that the author, John Bunyan, was teaching a profound truth. The man was saved when he entered the gate (his sins were forgiven), but it was not until he looked at the cross through his newly opened eyes that he had a fuller understanding of the atonement of Jesus Christ. It was then that the *burden* of his sin was removed.

There are many believers today who struggle with not feeling assured of their salvation. Though true believers, they are easily discouraged because they do not yet fully understand, at the deepest level, how gracious and merciful God their Savior is. They do not understand the full meaning of Christ's atonement. If we are to avoid giving in to the temptation to become discouraged, we must train our minds to meditate on who God is as the only God, our Savior through Jesus Christ.

Second, when facing potentially discouraging circumstances, we must remember *what God has*. At the end of verse 25 Jude declares that God has "glory, majesty, dominion and authority, before all time and now and forever. Amen." The word "be" in this verse is italicized ("to the only God our Savior . . . *be* glory . . ."), which means that it does not appear in the original text. I believe it does not belong in the English text as well because I believe Jude is saying that glory, majesty, dominion, and authority are what the only God our Savior through Jesus Christ *has*.

When we forget about what our God has, we can become discouraged. How glorious is our God? Consider these thoughts from the Scripture:

> O Lord, our Lord, how majestic is Your name in all
>    the earth,
> Who have displayed Your splendor above the heavens!
>    (Ps. 8:1)

> For Your lovingkindness is great to the heavens and
>    Your truth to the clouds.
> Be exalted above the heavens, O God; let Your glory
>    be above all the earth. (Ps. 57:10–11)

> For Your lovingkindness is great above the heavens,
>    and Your truth reaches to the skies. (Ps. 108:4)

> The Lord is high above all nations; His glory is above
>    the heavens.

Who is like the LORD our God, who is enthroned on
    high,
Who humbles Himself to behold the things that are
    in heaven and in the earth? (Ps. 113:4–6)

For as the heavens are higher than the earth,
So are My ways higher than your ways and My
    thoughts than your thoughts. (Isa. 55:9)

As glorious and majestic as God's creation is, it is but a small reflection of the glory and majesty of our God.

There is a passage in Isaiah 40 that I find especially compelling as a description of the awesome glory of God. Verse 12 asks, "Who has measured the waters in the hollow of His hand, and marked off the heavens by the span, and calculated the dust of the earth by the measure, and weighed the mountains in a balance and the hills in a pair of scales?" These are metaphors, of course, because God is a spirit and does not have a body as we do, but they tell us something of how big God really is. It is awesome to think that all the water of the earth could fit in the hollow of God's hand, and that the universe—which is infinite to us—is shorter than the length of God's hand.

Psalm 33:8 declares, "Let all the earth fear the LORD; let all the inhabitants of the world stand in awe of Him." Most of us do not do enough of that. We are too busy to stand still before our Creator and meditate on His glory and majesty. But in Psalm 46:10 God says, "Be still, and know that I am God; I will be exalted among the nations, I will be exalted in the earth!" (NKJV).

Moses needed to be reminded of this when he became greatly discouraged in his role as leader of the Israelites. He had just returned from Mount Sinai after receiving the first tablets of stone. When he came down into the camp of the Israelites, he found them worshipping and sacrificing to a golden calf that Aaron, Moses' assistant, had helped them make. After dealing with the people's sin, praying earnestly for their forgiveness, and pleading with God to not destroy them completely, Moses was understandably discouraged about his role as their leader. He pleaded with God, "Now therefore, I pray You, if I have found favor in Your sight, let me know Your ways that I may know You, so that I may find favor in Your sight. Consider too, that this nation is Your people" (Ex. 33:13). God replied to Moses, "My presence shall go with you, and I will give you rest" (33:14). The Lord reassured Moses that he would never have to do anything by himself or in his own strength.

Moses was not yet satisfied, however, and pressed God for further assurance of His help. He implored God, "I pray You, show me Your glory!" (33:18). God responded by telling Moses that though He could not show Moses His face, "for no man can see Me and live," He would allow Moses to see a small portion of His back (33:19–23). When Moses came down from the mountain after what must have been the most amazing experience of his life, his face shone so brightly that he had to wear a veil in the presence of the Israelites (34:29–30).

God is so glorious that if we in our present bodies were to see His full glory and majesty, we would be disintegrated in His presence. Even the seraphim, who are sinless creatures, always cover their faces and their feet in the presence of God

(Isa. 6:2). Our God is *truly awesome*, and in times of discouragement, we need to reflect on His glory and majesty.

We also need to reflect on the fact that He has dominion and authority over everything. Jesus declared, "All authority has been given to Me in heaven and on earth" (Matt. 28:18). Psalm 103:19 says, "The LORD has established His throne in the heavens, and His sovereignty rules over all." Psalm 115:3 teaches, "But our God is in the heavens; He does whatever He pleases."

Our God answers to no one. He is sovereign over the angels, over Satan, and over the demons. Hebrews 1:14 asks, "Are [the angels] not all ministering spirits, sent out to render service for the sake of those who will inherit salvation?" God commands His angels and they obey Him perfectly, absolutely, exclusively, and continuously. Satan is restrained by God as well, and could do no more to Job than God allowed him to do: "Behold, all that he has is in your power, only do not put forth your hand on him" (Job 1:12). We need to remember the extent of God's dominion and authority.

Bunyan illustrated this idea in *The Pilgrim's Progress* when Christian was walking along and encountered two men, Timorous and Mistrust, running in the opposite direction. As these two men passed Christian, they warned him to turn around and go back because there were lions up ahead. Hearing this, Christian was tempted to turn back, but at that point someone else came along. This person said there were lions but added that those lions were securely chained.

The truth here is that God has Satan and his demons on a chain as well. They can do only what God permits them to do and *no more*. We tend to forget that and become frightened by the thought that there are uncontrolled evil beings all around, ready to do us harm. That can be a very discouraging thought! It is not a thought based on truth, however, and if we want to avoid discouragement, we need to focus our minds on truth.

We need to remember again not only that God is in control of all heavenly powers, but that He is our Savior. In other words, He has only good in mind for us. "If God is for us, who is against us?" (Rom. 8:31). In Jeremiah 29:11 God said, "For I know the plans that I have for you, . . . plans for welfare and not for calamity to give you a future and a hope."

This God, our Savior, has all dominion and authority over all powers on earth as well as in heaven. Proverbs 21:1 teaches, "The king's heart is like channels of water in the hand of the LORD; He turns it wherever He wishes." In Daniel 4:35 Nebuchadnezzar declared, "All the inhabitants of the earth are accounted as nothing, but He does according to His will in the host of heaven and among the inhabitants of earth; and no one can ward off His hand or say to Him, 'What have You done?' " There is no one on earth that can call God to account for anything.

We return to Isaiah 40, where verse 15 says, "Behold, the nations are like a drop from a bucket, and are regarded as a speck of dust on the scales." A speck of dust, when we are weighing much more significant items, is not even worth brushing off; that is what God calls all the nations of the earth. All together, they are an insignificant speck in His sight, and He has complete dominion over them.

God is also sovereign over the circumstances of our lives. Joseph told his brothers, who had intended to harm him, "As for you, you meant evil against me, but God meant it for good in order to bring about this present result" (Gen. 50:20). Proverbs 21:30 teaches, "There is no wisdom and no understanding and no counsel against the LORD." And, of course, Romans 8:28 promises, "And we know that God causes all things to work together for good to those who love God."

God has dominion and authority over all His creation as well. He causes the sun to shine (Matt. 5:45) and the rain to fall (Amos 4:7). He controls the lion's mouth (Dan. 6:22). Job acknowledged, "It is God who removes the mountains, they know not how, when He overturns them in His anger; who shakes the earth out of its place, and its pillars tremble; who commands the sun not to shine, and sets a seal upon the stars; who alone stretches out the heavens and tramples down the waves of the sea" (Job 9:5–8).

When we lived in California, we experienced firsthand the Lord shaking the earth out of its place. The earthquake of 1994 was the most frightening thing we have ever experienced in terms of the forces of nature, and it was a great comfort to know that God was in control. My wife was teaching kindergarten at the time, and when the children in her class became frightened by the aftershocks (which continued for days afterward), she calmly explained to them that "God was just settling the earth."

It was not until the principal was in her classroom during a later aftershock that she realized what a comfort this was to her students. As the principal attempted to comfort the students himself, expecting them to be quite frightened by the shaking, several of them reassured him, "Mr. Duncan, don't worry; it's just God settling the earth." Those kids understood that God is in control of the forces of nature, and they were able to minister to their principal at a time when he expected to comfort them.

God has all glory, majesty, dominion, and authority; that is a powerfully encouraging truth. Not only that, but Jude said that He has it "before all time and now and forever" (v. 25). Throughout history, there have been rulers with immense power and prestige. When Alexander the Great was twenty-nine years of age, he had conquered all the known world. At that point, it is said that he sat down and wept because there was nothing left to conquer. Alexander the Great might have been great on the earth while he lived, but, as we know, he died and others took his place.

Numerous great kings have reigned on the earth—Nebuchadnezzar, the pharaohs of Egypt, the emperors of Rome—and all of them have died. Nations rise and fall, rulers come and go, but our God reigns! Whatever the military capacity of a nation, even a nation as strong as ours, God's strength is infinitely beyond it. "Some boast in chariots and some in horses, but we will boast in the name of the LORD, our God. They have bowed down and fallen, but we have risen and stood upright" (Ps. 20:7–8).

## REMEMBERING WHAT GOD CAN DO

We must remember who God is and what God has, and third, when facing potentially discouraging circumstances, we must remember *what God can do*. In verse 24 Jude said, "Now to Him who is able to keep you from stumbling, and to make you stand in the presence of His glory blameless with great joy." "Our God is able!" That should be the constant heart-cry of every true believer.

The Scripture is full of reminders of how able our God is and what He is able to do. Second Corinthians 9:8 says, "And God is able to make all grace abound to you, so that always having all sufficiency in everything, you may have an abundance for every good deed." Ephesians 3:20 ascribes glory to "Him who is able to do far more abundantly beyond all that we ask or think, according to the power that works within us." Do we really believe that we cannot even begin to imagine how much God can do in us and for us?

Philippians 4:19 promises, "And my God will supply all your needs according to His riches in glory in Christ Jesus." Regardless of our circumstances or disabilities, God can supply all our needs. Do we really believe that? Philippians 3:21 notes that Jesus will "transform the body of our humble state into conformity with the body of His glory, by the exertion of the power that He has even to subject all things to Himself." God is able to transform our corrupt, decaying, weak bodies into glorious bodies, and He has promised to do so someday.

Hebrews 7:25 declares, "Therefore He is able also to save forever those who draw near to God through Him, since He always lives to make intercession for them." He is able to fulfill all His promises: "For as many as are the promises of God, in Him they are yes; therefore also through Him is our Amen to the glory of God through us" (2 Cor. 1:20). Jeremiah 32:17 reminds, "Ah Lord GOD! Behold, You have made the heavens and the earth by Your great power and by Your outstretched arm! Nothing is too difficult for You."

Jude reminds us that our God is able to "make [us] stand in the presence of His glory blameless with great joy." In other words, He is able to finish the work that He began in us of making us like Christ, holy and blameless in His sight. By Christ's redemptive work on the cross, we are no longer under condemnation (we are blameless of sin), but we are not yet perfected as we will be one day. In heaven, we will no longer be working out our salvation (Phil. 2:12) or struggling with sin as we do now (Rom. 7:21–25).

Not only that, but our God, who is going to make us stand in His presence, promises to give us "great joy" as well (Jude 25). David said, "In Your presence is fullness of joy; in Your right hand there are pleasures forever" (Ps. 16:11). We have never known the kind of joy that we will experience in God's presence. In fact, our finite minds cannot even imagine it.

Still further, Jude explained that our God is "able to keep [us] from stumbling" (v. 24). As we all know, it is not an easy thing to live for Christ in this sinful world. We are surrounded by potentially discouraging things: apostasy and heresy in the church, strife and contention among people who profess Christ, perversions and evils of both pagans and those who call themselves Christians, and hard-hearted people who are not willing to listen to the truth. The temptation to become discouraged can be great. Yet God promises to keep us from stumbling. The word that is translated "stumbling" is the Greek word *aptaistos* (meaning "falling") and is derived from the Greek word *ptaiō*, which means "to err, sin, fail of salvation." When Jude said that God was able to keep us from stumbling, he was teaching two things. First, he was teaching that what God started in us at salvation, He will complete. "For I am confident of this very thing, that He who began a good work in you will perfect it until the day of Christ Jesus" (Phil. 1:6). Second, Jude was teaching that God is able to and will keep us from stumbling in sin *even now*. Thus Romans 8:37 says, "But in all these things we overwhelmingly conquer through Him who loved us." And 2 Corinthians 2:14 exults, "But thanks be to God, who always leads us in triumph in Christ." Though we are completely unable to avoid sin by our own strength and will, God is able to keep us from sin by His strength and according to His will.

That is God's solution to the problem of discouragement: remembering who He is, what He has, and what He is able to do. Though some of us have known these truths for many, many years, the key to this solution is not in knowing, but in *remembering, reflecting on, believing, and applying them.* In other words, these things that we know must be stirred up in our hearts so that they are fresh in our minds and at the forefront of our thoughts. These truths must be more than things that we know; they must be what control us.

In 1 Timothy 4:7 Paul exhorted Timothy and all other believers to "discipline yourself for the purpose of godliness." Godliness is not merely what we do (good deeds are an expression of our godliness), but an expression of who we are. The Greek word *eusebeia*, which is translated "godliness," derives from the Greek word *eusebēs*, which means "to be devout." Godliness describes a life that is God-centered. People who are godly have God at the center of their thinking; they look at the world through God rather than looking at God through the world.

Truly, as Paul said, we must *train ourselves* to think this way because it is not the natural inclination of our minds. If we are serious about dealing with discouragement—whether discouragement that we are already experiencing, or circumstances that are tempting us to become discouraged—we must be willing to follow the instruction of God, through Jude, for solving this problem. We must make every effort to focus our minds constantly on who God is, what He has, and what He is able to do. These are the great truths that will provide the cure for discouragements and help us to truly glorify God and enjoy Him forever. Let us meditate constantly on the greatness and grace of our God, and let us pray that our great God will firmly impress these truths about Himself upon our hearts and minds so that we might glorify and magnify His name and experience the blessings He wants us to have in the present life.

## APPLICATION

1. On what particular problem does this chapter focus?

2. The material in this chapter is mainly based on Jude 24–25. Write out these verses and add them to the list of verses you are working on memorizing.

3. Describe the potentially discouraging circumstances of the people to whom Jude originally wrote these verses. Look carefully at verses 3–23.

4. Describe a discouraging time that you have experienced or are experiencing. What were or are the circumstances? How did these circumstances affect you? What did you do or are you doing? What were or are you thinking and feeling?

5. What is the first thing mentioned in this chapter that we must do if we are to prevent and overcome discouragement?

6. In particular, what does Jude tell us to remember about who God is that will help us to prevent and overcome discouragement?

7. Why will knowing, believing, and meditating on these truths about who God *is* be so encouraging in the midst of difficult circumstances?

8. What is the second thing mentioned in this chapter that we must do if we are to prevent and overcome discouragement?

9. In particular, what does Jude tell us to remember about what God has that will help us to prevent and overcome discouragement?

10. Why will knowing, believing, and meditating on these truths about what God *has* be so encouraging in the midst of difficult circumstances?

11. What is the third thing mentioned in this chapter that we must do if we are to prevent and overcome discouragement?

12. In particular, what does Jude tell us to remember about what God can do that will help us to prevent and overcome discouragement?

13. Why will knowing, believing, and meditating on these truths about what God *can do* be so encouraging in the midst of difficult circumstances?

14. How can the information presented in this chapter be of practical help in your own life and in your ministry to others?

# 12

## HOPELESSNESS

What three character qualities are most important in the Christian life? If we could ask the apostle Paul, I believe that his answer would be the well-known triad: faith, hope, and love. In 1 Corinthians 13:13 Paul wrote, "But now faith, hope, love, abide these three." These three are mentioned together in several other places as well, including Ephesians 1:15–18 and Colossians 1:4–5. To the Thessalonians he wrote, "constantly bearing in mind your work of *faith* and labor of *love* and steadfastness of *hope* in our Lord Jesus Christ in the presence of our God and Father" (1 Thess. 1:3).

It is apparent from a careful study of the Scripture that these three qualities are most important in the Christian life because everything else flows out of them. Faith is important because it is the means through which we are saved: "For by grace you have been saved through faith; and that not of yourselves, it is the gift of God" (Eph. 2:8). As believers, we have been justified by faith so that we can have peace with God (Rom. 5:1). In fact, without faith it is impossible for us to please God in any way (Heb. 11:6).

Love is important because without it, according to the Word of God, we are nothing (1 Cor. 13:1–3). In 1 Timothy 1:5 Paul said, "But the goal of our instruction is love from a pure heart and a good conscience and a sincere faith." The apostle John said that love is an essential evidence of our faith and obedience: "Beloved, let us love one another, for love is from God; and everyone who loves is born of God and knows God" (1 John 4:7); and "this is love, that we walk according to His commandments" (2 John 1:6).

To be sure, faith and love are important elements of the Christian life. This is undoubtedly why they are the subjects of much preaching and teaching, but what about hope? Hope is frequently mentioned in the Bible, but how often do we hear a sermon or read a book on the subject of hope? Sadly, hope is largely neglected in Christian teaching, even though the Bible has much to say about its importance in our lives.

## HOPE IS VITALLY IMPORTANT

Why is hope so important to believers? Hope is mentioned throughout Scripture, and each description illustrates a different aspect of its importance. In Hebrews 6:17–19 hope is described as *an anchor for our souls.* "This hope we have as an anchor of the soul, a hope both sure and steadfast and one which enters within the veil" (6:19). Hope keeps our souls on course by providing stability and consistency. It keeps us from getting tossed about in doctrine by heresy and tossed about in morality by temptations to sin.

According to 1 Thessalonians 4:13, hope *prevents us from being overwhelmed by sorrow*: "so that you will not grieve as do the rest who have no hope." When unbelievers lose a loved one, they have sorrow without hope. As believers, when we lose a loved one who is also a believer, we have hope because we know that we will see that person again in heaven. Likewise, in distressing circumstances we have hope because we know that God is working all things together for good. Hope keeps us from being overwhelmed by sorrow.

Hope *gives us great boldness,* according to 2 Corinthians 3:12: "Therefore having such a hope, we use great boldness in our speech." We can be courageous in sharing the gospel and in ministering to and serving others because of the hope that we have. We can declare the truth of the Scripture with boldness and surety, even in the face of opposition, because of hope.

Our hope also *results in gladness and praise.* According to Proverbs 10:28, "The hope of the righteous is gladness, but the expectation of the wicked perishes." And Psalm 16:9 says, "Therefore my heart is glad, and my glory rejoices; my flesh also will rest in hope" (NKJV). In Romans 5:3–5 Paul said that we can experience joy and gladness in times of trial because of hope. "And not only this, but we also exult in our tribulations, knowing that tribulation brings about perseverance . . . and proven character, hope; and hope does not disappoint." We can have gladness in trial because, though the pain and suffering are real, we glory in God.

Hope *allows us to be patient.* Galatians 5:5 says, "For we by the Spirit, by faith, are waiting for the hope of righteousness." We can wait patiently for what God has promised us because we have confidence that He will bring it to pass. Hope also *produces obedience.* Hebrews 11 says that Abraham and others obeyed God because they had faith, but also because of the hope that they had in God's promises: "All these died in faith, without receiving the promises, but having seen them and having welcomed them from a distance . . ." (Heb. 11:13).

Hope *helps us to deny ourselves.* During his ministry Paul and his companions were afflicted, perplexed, persecuted, struck down, and constantly delivered over to death for Jesus' sake (2 Cor. 4:8–11). Despite all this he wrote, "But if we are afflicted, it is for your comfort and salvation; . . . and our hope for you is firmly grounded, knowing that as you are sharers of our sufferings, so also you are sharers of our comfort" (2 Cor. 1:6–7). Paul denied himself because he had hope for the salvation of others.

Hope *produces godliness.* In 1 John 3:1–2 the apostle John said that we are sons of God, and because we are sons of God, "we will be like Him." Then he said, "And everyone who has this hope fixed on Him purifies himself, just as He is pure" (3:3). Our hope produces purity—holiness and godliness. First Thessalonians 1:3 also makes this connection between hope and holiness. Paul praised his readers because their hope had produced in them steadfastness, so that they were able to do labors of love and works of faith.

Romans 15:13 says that hope is a *source of peace and joy:* "Now may the God of hope fill you with all joy and peace in believing, so that you will abound in hope by the power of the Holy Spirit." David connected hope with peace in Psalm 16:9, "My flesh also will rest in hope" (NKJV), and Paul connected hope to joy in Romans 12:12, "rejoicing in hope, persevering in tribulation, devoted to prayer."

Hope is a *source of evangelistic opportunity.* First Peter 3:15 urges, "But sanctify Christ as Lord in your hearts, always being ready to make a defense to everyone who asks you to give an account for the hope that is in you, yet with gentleness and reverence." We live in a hopeless world, and when unbelievers see us rejoicing in the midst of turmoil, they are going to ask us how we can have such hope. As ambassadors of Christ, we must be always ready to answer.

For instance, I took my wife to a jewelry store on our thirty-eighth anniversary to buy her something special. The salesman gave us a wonderful opportunity to witness when he asked us how we had stayed together for so many years. My wife and I were able to share with this man how we had come to know and love Jesus Christ. As we spoke, the salesman listened with great interest, visibly affected by our testimony of hope in Christ.

Later, I stopped by the store again to invite him to church. As we talked, it became apparent that the difference that he noticed in our lives—our peace and joy and hope—made him want to know more about what we believed. He asked questions and I was able to share the gospel with him. Without seeking it out or even expecting it to come, I was able to evangelize because of the hope that my wife and I had in Christ and evidenced during that first encounter.

Lastly, a lack of hope *leads to weakness*—both physically and spiritually. In Lamentations 3:18 Jeremiah mourned, "So

I say, 'My strength has perished, and so has my hope from the LORD.' " God used similar language with regard to the children of Israel, though from a positive perspective, through the prophet Isaiah: "You were tired out by the length of your road, yet you did not say, 'It is hopeless.' You found renewed strength, therefore you did not faint" (Isa. 57:10). Because the people had hope, they had strength to finish their journey.

As the Scripture has shown, hope is a multifaceted quality. An attitude of hope in the hearts of believers is essential because it is productive and practical in so many ways. It is an anchor for our souls, prevents overwhelming sorrow, gives us boldness, and produces in us gladness and praise. Hope helps us to wait patiently for the Lord, produces obedience, enables us to deny ourselves, and is critical to producing godliness and holiness in our lives. Hope results in joy and peace, can open up evangelistic opportunities, and gives us strength.

Therefore, if we are weak in any of these areas—stability, boldness, gladness, obedience, godliness—it may be an indication of a fundamental lack of hope in our lives. Our struggles are often just symptoms of a larger problem. As a biblical counselor, when I encounter someone who is struggling with any of these things, I immediately think that this person probably lacks hope, and I work toward overcoming the symptoms *and* fostering hope.

## WHAT HAPPENS WHEN PEOPLE LACK HOPE

To prevent these problems in the first place, it is important that we as believers actively pursue this quality of hope in our lives. Consider two examples of what happens when believers lack hope. The first comes from Numbers 13:25–14:4, which records the time when Moses sent twelve men into Canaan to spy out the land. When the spies returned, they reported to everyone what they had seen. Ten of them said that the land was indeed flowing with milk and honey, as God had promised, but it was also full of strong people in fortified cities. In fact, according to the ten, it was pointless to even try to enter the land and take possession of it. "We are not able to go up against the people, for they are too strong for us" (13:31).

The people heard this report and were very upset because they believed the words of the ten spies who despaired. "Then all the congregation lifted up their voices and cried, and the people wept that night" (14:1). They immediately decided that it was better to return to Egypt than to go into this land that God had promised them. "So they said to one another, 'Let us appoint a leader and return to Egypt' " (14:4). In other words, the people lost hope because of the spies' bad report. They had no boldness and no will to obey because they lacked hope.

The second example comes from John Bunyan's *The Pilgrim's Progress*. At one point in Bunyan's story, Christian and Hopeful have just passed by the Crystal River (a place of refreshment and blessing by God) when the path that they are taking becomes rough. Despite Hopeful's misgivings that they might lose sight of the main path, they decide to leave the main path for a side path that appears to parallel the other, but runs through easier terrain.

Soon they encounter trouble. Night falls, a violent storm breaks over them, and the water beside the path begins to rise quickly. "Hopeful groaned to himself, 'If I had only kept on my way.' " As they lie down to sleep, Christian and Hopeful discuss their troubles a bit before succumbing to weariness. In the morning Giant Despair, the owner of the land on which they have been trespassing, finds them and wakes them up to ask what they are doing on his land. The two companions answer that they are on a journey and have lost their way.

Giant Despair declares them to have committed an offense against him by being on his property and demands that they follow him to his house, Doubting Castle. In the castle they are thrown into a dungeon without food, light, or hope of escape. Soon Giant Despair comes to them in the dungeon (at the urging of his wife, Distrust) and counsels Christian and Hopeful to kill themselves because there is no hope for them. At this, Christian says to Hopeful, "Oh, my brother! What shall we do? The life we are now living is miserable, and as for me, I don't know whether it is best to live like this or to die on the spot. My soul would rather choose to die than to live, and the grave will be easier for me than this dungeon. Shall we live our lives in bondage to this Giant?"

Christian had fallen into despair and depression because he had lost hope. When people lose hope, they can enter into such depression that they contemplate suicide or other terrible sins. As believers, we face this danger as well if we do not pursue and maintain hope in our lives.

In contrast to these examples, consider the words of David in Psalm 38. In verses 10–12 David described his present circumstances:

My heart throbs, my strength fails me;
And the light of my eyes, even that has gone from me.

My loved ones and my friends stand aloof from my
    plague;
And my kinsmen stand afar off.
Those who seek my life lay snares for me;
And those who seek to injure me have threatened
    destruction,
And they devise treachery all day long.

David was clearly in a time of distress. His health was poor, his friends and family were abandoning him, and his enemies were taking every opportunity to abuse him. In the face of this difficulty, David's response is this (vv. 13–15):

But I, like a deaf man, do not hear;
And I am like a mute man who does not open his
    mouth.
Yes, I am like a man who does not hear,
And in whose mouth are no arguments.
For I hope in You, O LORD;
You will answer, O Lord my God.

David responded by being quiet. He did not complain about physical weakness or about being abandoned. He did not listen to the ridicule of his enemies, think about how to respond to them, or verbally defend himself.

Why was David able to remain quiet? He was able to do this because he had hope. He believed that it was better to turn it all over to the Lord and let the Lord handle it than to become anxious and despair. He believed the words that he had written in Psalm 37: "Commit your way to the LORD, trust also in

Him, and He will do it. He will bring forth your righteous-ness as the light and your judgment as the noonday" (37:5–6).

Because hope is so evidently important to the Christian life—helping us to respond properly in difficult situations and keeping us from many spiritual and physical harms caused by a lack of hope—it seems necessary to consider two questions. One, what is true biblical hope? And two, how is this hope developed and maintained in the life of a believer?

The Bible indicates that unbelievers sometimes have a kind of hope, but it is a false, empty hope. "So are the paths of all who forget God; and the hope of the godless will per-ish, whose confidence is fragile, and whose trust a spider's web" (Job 8:13–14). Their hope is based on earthly things, which are ultimately as transitory and powerless as they are. "When a wicked man dies, his expectation will perish, and the hope of strong men perishes" (Prov. 11:7). The hope of the unbe-liever is really an "I hope so" rather than a true hope.

What, then, is true hope? In the remainder of this chap-ter, we will consider several aspects of true biblical hope, as well as how each of these aspects can be developed and main-tained. The first and foundational aspect of true hope is that it is possible only for those who have been born again. Until a person has repented of sin and professed faith in Jesus Christ for salvation, one is incapable of knowing true hope. Eph-esians 2:12 describes unbelievers in this way: "separate from Christ . . . and strangers to the covenants of promise, having no hope and without God in the world."

When a person professes Christ, only then is he or she able to know the "living hope" described in 1 Peter 1:3: "Blessed be the God and Father of our Lord Jesus Christ, who according to His great mercy has caused us to be born again to a living hope through the resurrection of Jesus Christ from the dead." Indeed, it is our privilege as believers to experience this living hope and to be recipients of all the things that God has promised in His Word to give to those who love Him. The promises of God are the birthright of all that are born of Him.

A woman came for counseling some time ago and described to me the life of immorality, deception, and failure that she had been living. She had seduced older men, been involved in prostitution, had two illegitimate children, had three abortions, and recently learned that she had cancer. She admitted that she had no hope because her life was such a mess. Honestly, the counselor had to agree with her about having no hope. As a sinner, she had no hope. However, the good news of the gospel is that anyone—no matter how sinful—can be forgiven and can know true hope in Christ. No one is beyond the reach of God's grace.

God's grace is the instrument of our salvation, and it is also the only means by which we can experience the true hope of God in our lives. Second Thessalonians 2:16–17 says, "Now may our Lord Jesus Christ Himself and God our Father, who has loved us and given us eternal comfort and good hope by grace, comfort and strengthen your hearts in every good work and word." Just as our salvation is not based on personal merit or works of righteousness, neither is our hope. Hope is entirely a gift of God's grace.

## How True Hope Is Developed and Maintained

This true hope, made possible through salvation and the grace of God, is increased by a deepening relationship with Jesus Christ. In 1 Timothy 1:1 Paul said that Jesus Christ *is our hope*. Ultimately, our hope is not really in statements or rules or even doctrinal truths, but in Jesus Christ Himself. As we develop our relationship with Him, it is He—through the Holy Spirit—who sustains and increases our hope.

I once counseled a woman who had attempted suicide several times. She had struggled with depression since her teenage years. She had tried psychiatry and medication, but nothing had worked. Although she claimed to be a Christian, she had pushed Christ completely out of her life. She was not reading her Bible or going to church, and she was neglecting her duties as a wife.

As we talked, I began by telling her that because only Christ could really help her, we would focus on her relationship with Him; what she needed to do was to think biblically, to really love Christ, and to obey His Word. Though it was an unusually short time, in about twelve weeks she was a changed person—by God's grace. She wrote me a note several months after our sessions ended, expressing her thanks and telling me how God continued to bless her. Her relationship with Christ had been restored, and she was able to have true hope in her Lord.

A vital, growing relationship with Christ is the foundation of true hope. The second aspect of true hope, according to the Word of God, is a *confident, certain expectation of good that is based on the promises of God*. True hope is not based on man's opinions or predictions, or man's strength. True hope is firmly planted in a rock-solid promise of God. For example, Titus 1:2 says that we have the "hope of eternal life, which God, who cannot lie, promised long ages ago." Our hope in eternal life is true hope.

Indeed, every promise in the Bible is something for which we can have true hope. We can have hope for ultimate good in every situation: "And we know that God causes all things to work together for good to those who love God, to those who are called according to His purpose" (Rom. 8:28). We can have hope for grace: "And God is able to make all grace abound to you, so that always having all sufficiency in everything, you may have an abundance for every good deed" (2 Cor. 9:8). We can have hope for the provision of all our needs: "And my God will supply all your needs according to His riches in glory in Christ Jesus" (Phil. 4:19).

If one aspect of true hope is confidence in the promises of God, then part of developing and maintaining true hope in our lives must be *meditation on the promises of God*. The promises of God, and His absolute ability to keep them, are critical to true hope. In my library I have a book entitled *All the Promises of God*. The author of this book, through careful study of the Bible, has found and listed some 3,500 promises of God. There is a promise in the Bible for every situation and need that any believer could ever encounter on this earth, but we must know those promises in order to hope in them.

In our earlier example, Christian and Hopeful did not remain in the dungeon of Doubting Castle forever, and neither did they commit suicide. They got out, and Bunyan indicates that there were three things that God used to bring Christian out of his depression. These three things are the next three steps to developing and maintaining true hope in our lives.

First, in the dungeon of Doubting Castle, Hopeful began to counsel his friend Christian. So also, God often uses the wise, loving counsel and encouragement of fellow believers to help us in a time of despair.

Second, Christian and Hopeful began to pray. They turned to God for help instead of dwelling on their circumstances. Likewise, the Scripture calls us to pray for help:

> This poor man cried, and the LORD heard him
> And saved him out of all his troubles. (Ps. 34:6)

> Call upon Me in the day of trouble;
> I shall rescue you, and you will honor Me. (Ps. 50:15)

> Cast your burden upon the LORD and He will sustain
>     you;
> He will never allow the righteous to be shaken. (Ps.
>     55:22)

Third, after praying all night, Christian suddenly remembered that he had a key in his pocket called "Promise." He immediately surmised that this key would open any lock in the castle. When it easily opened the dungeon door, he used it again on the next door—though he found that one to be a little harder. In fact, each new door and gate was a little harder to open than the one before it, but each one eventually opened when the key was used with determination. Finally, Christian and Hopeful reached the outer Iron Gate of the castle. This last gate was especially stubborn, but they were able to open it also with the key.

What Bunyan so well described in this part of his story is what often happens to us when we are under the control of despair and depression. Though we have the key in our pocket—the promises of God—we forget about it in our time of need. When we finally remember that needed promise, meditate on it and believe it, we are able to move out of the control of despair. Then, something else happens—we reach a new door that is harder to open—and we feel imprisoned again.

At this point, we may be tempted to say that God's promises do not work. I often hear that from people whom I am counseling. They tried the key once, but now there is another, more difficult door. Instead of renewing their determination and using the key again, they simply give up on the key entirely and begin to look for help elsewhere: worldly wisdom, psychology, drugs, or some kind of spiritual wizardry.

Bunyan's story illustrates for us the truth that the only thing we need for each new door (each new difficulty) is the same key (God's promises) that worked the first time. God the Holy Spirit uses His promises to maintain our hope, but these promises can be brought to our minds only if they are already there. In other words, we have the power and the responsibility to put the key in our pocket. We must be faithful in meditating on and memorizing the promises of God so that they are hidden away in our hearts, ready to be used whenever trouble comes.

The third aspect of true hope is closely related to the second. True hope depends on a *diligent, consistent, and accurate exegesis of the Word of God.* The promises of God are revealed in His Word, but we must always seek to know and understand them correctly. In Luke 24 the story is told of two disciples walking to Emmaus. Jesus had risen from the dead, and it had only just been reported to His disciples, though many did not yet believe it was true. These two were discussing all the things that had happened when Jesus, whom they did not recognize, joined them on the road. The Bible says that they had lost hope, but as Jesus talked with them and instructed them, their hearts burned within them (24:13–33).

In my experience as a biblical counselor, I have witnessed this same kind of thing many times. People come to me who have lost hope, and as I open the Word of God to them and apply it to their lives, their hope increases. True believers love the Word of God, and their spirit will respond when it is accurately opened to them.

It is important for us to correctly exegete the Word of God because we can be easily disappointed by hoping in misinterpreted promises. I once counseled a woman who declared that she was giving up Christianity because she had claimed a promise from the Word and it had not proven true. It turned out that she had incorrectly used Matthew 18:19 as a promise for answered prayer when in fact it is a promise relating to church discipline. Because she had not correctly understood the Scripture in the first place, she had placed her hope in something that did not accurately represent the truth of God's Word.

In the same way, we need to be wary of teachers who incorrectly interpret the Word. I have counseled many people who lost hope because of false promises that they were given by teachers of "Name It, Claim It," "Health and Wealth," and other false theologies. They based their hope on a misinterpretation of the Word of God and were so disappointed that they questioned the truth of their faith. We must learn to think biblically so that we can understand correctly for ourselves and judge accurately the teaching of others regarding God's promises.

Fourth, true hope is *comprehensive in focus.* It focuses on both the present and the future, on all the facts of a situation (both negative and positive), on corporate more than personal blessings, and on spiritual more than material things. In other words, true hope has an other-centered view of the world, not a me-centered view. A true believer hopes for and rejoices in the advance of God's kingdom at whatever personal cost.

Fifth, true hope *depends on a biblical view of personal responsibility.* Jerry Bridges, in his book *Discipline of Grace,* gives the illustration of an airplane being like the Christian life. Though some planes are designed to fly without one of their engines if need be, no plane can fly without two wings. Two wings are an absolute necessity; practically speaking, one wing is the same as no wings. In the Christian life, those two essential wings are dependence on God and the discipline of effort on our part. In other words, we must depend completely on God, but we must also make every effort toward obedience.

This is true also in terms of hope. We have already said that true hope depends completely on God for all things. At the same time, however, true hope recognizes our personal responsibility to obey God in all things. We are responsible to continue in prayer, to read the Word, to discipline our minds, and to act biblically in every situation. It is not enough to say simply, "I've given it all to God," and then step back and wait for something to happen. We must give it all to God *and* do all God asks us to do in pursuing holiness.

Finally, true hope is *developed and sustained by the encouragement of other believers.* Just as Hopeful encouraged Christian in *The Pilgrim's Progress,* we need the close, loving fellowship and encouragement of other believers who are mature in their faith and can keep us on track. Hebrews 10:24–25 teaches, "And let us consider how to stimulate one another to love and good deeds, not forsaking our own assembling together, as is the habit of some, but encouraging one another; and all the more as you see the day drawing near."

I have found that among the people I have counseled, many of those who have experienced deep discouragement and depression were people who were isolated from others. They had not made themselves accountable or received encouragement and instruction from a godly friend. The Bible commands us to be that kind of friend to one another, and it is important that we seek out those kinds of friends so that they can help us to recognize and deal with our sin before it becomes a serious, debilitating problem in our lives.

Friends, we have been given a *living hope* in Christ Jesus. We have been called by God to experience true hope. "There is one body and one Spirit, just as also you were called in one hope of your calling" (Eph. 4:4). If we desire to maintain and increase that true hope in our lives, then we must be diligent to pursue it. We must seek to deepen our relationship with our Lord, meditate on His promises, understand correctly His Word, be comprehensive in our focus, accept our personal responsibility, and pursue godly relationships with others.

Is your life characterized by an attitude of hope? Do you stand out from the crowd of gloom and doom that is all around us in this world, or do you blend in? Do others wonder what makes you different? Can you say with the hymn writer, "My hope is built on nothing less than Jesus' blood and righteousness"? With Paul, "I pray that the eyes of your heart may be enlightened, so that you will know what is the hope of His calling, what are the riches of the glory of His inheritance in the saints, and what is the surpassing greatness of His power toward us who believe" (Eph. 1:18–19).

## APPLICATION

1. What is true hope? How would you define it?

2. Who are the only people who can have a true hope? Why?

3. How is true hope increased in your life?

4. How is true hope evidenced in your life?

5. What is true hope based on, and how is it developed and sustained?

6. Give an example of a time in your life when a promise of God was a tremendous encouragement to you. What was the promise?

7. Why is a careful, correct exegesis of Scripture such an important part of developing and sustaining true hope?

Why is misinterpreting Scripture a detriment to developing and sustaining true hope?

8. Why does developing and sustaining a true hope require accepting personal responsibility for your actions, thoughts, feelings, and reactions?

9. Give an example of a time when another believer encouraged you. What was done or said that helped you develop and sustain a hopeful attitude?

10. Whom will you encourage this week, and how will you do it?

11. Select two verses mentioned in this chapter that were meaningful to you; write them out and work on memorizing them.

12. How can the information presented in this chapter be of practical help in your own life and in your ministry to others?

# INDEX OF SCRIPTURE

**Wayne A. Mack** (M.Div., Philadelphia Theological Seminary; D.Min., Westminster Theological Seminary) is adjunct professor of biblical counseling at The Master's College and director of Strengthening Ministries International. Mack is an executive board member of F.I.R.E. (Fellowship of Independent Reformed Evangelicals) and co-pastor of Grace Fellowship Church of the Lehigh Valley. He is a charter member and executive board member of the National Association of Nouthetic Counselors. Wayne is also a member of the board of directors of the missionary agency Publicacione Fara de Gracia. He conducts seminars and conferences around the world.

Mack has authored a number of books, including *Reaching the Ear of God*; *Strengthening Your Marriage*; *Your Family, God's Way*; *A Homework Manual for Biblical Living, vols. 1 and 2*; with David Swavely, *Life in the Father's House*; and with John MacArthur, *An Introduction to Biblical Counseling*. He and his wife Carol have four children and thirteen grandchildren. They live in the Lehigh Valley in Pennsylvania.